Best of Country Cookies

A cookie jarful of the country's best family favorites...selected from _over_ _34,000_ shared by subscribers in _Taste of Home's_ "Cookie of All Cookies" contest.

And the winner is... "_Mmm_minnesota Munchers", shown on our cover, entered by Marcia Severson of Hallock, Minnesota. See details on page 6.

Let the Baking Begin...

Here's a picture preview of this book's contents and some of the winning recipes in each category—family favorites to suit every taste and time schedule.

We Were Overwhelmed...page 6
The story behind the contest

Drop Cookies...page 18
Simple as dropping from a spoon

Cutout Classics...page 44
Fancy for fancier occasions

Shaped Specialties...page 52
Wide variety of types and shapes

Bars & Brownies...page 74
One-pan creations, cut 'n' serve

Refrigerator Favorites...page 90
Dough now, bake when convenient

Sandwich Cookies...page 96
Kids (of all ages) love 'em

Bake Sale Bonanza...page 102
Tasty batches for big groups

Quick & Easy Treats...page 108
Few ingredients, little baking

Looking for a certain cookie?
The index begins on page 112.

Editor: Julie Schnittka
Food Editor: Coleen Martin
Associate Food Editor: Corinne Willkomm
Senior Recipe Editor: Sue A. Jurack
Assistant Editors: Kristine Krueger, Jean Steiner
Art Director: Stephanie Marchese
Art Assistants: Maribeth Greinke, Ellen Lloyd, Claudia Wardius
Test Kitchen Home Economists: Judith Scholovich,
Anita Bukowski, Betty Reuter
Test Kitchen Assistant: Suzi Hampton
Photography: Scott Anderson, Glenn Thiesenhusen
Photo Studio Manager: Anne Schimmel
Publisher: Roy Reiman

© 1999, Reiman Publications, LLC
5400 S. 60th St., Greendale WI 53129
International Standard Book Number: 0-89821-260-X
Library of Congress Catalog Card Number: 99-70498
All rights reserved.
Printed in U.S.A.

The Story Behind the Search for the
'COOKIE OF ALL COOKIES'

"OH, MY, GOSH! This is absolutely *wonderful!*"

"I have to admit it…I've never tasted a cookie as good as this one. Even my grandmother's weren't *this* good!"

Those are the kind of comments we loved hearing as we tested and our subscribers tasted a half dozen cookie recipes per day at our company Visitor Center in downtown Greendale, Wisconsin.

It was part of the daily excitement for nearly a year as we conducted *Taste of Home's* National Cookie Recipe

RECIPES BY THE THOUSANDS! Over *34,000* entries poured in, overwhelming Food Editor Coleen Martin and the rest of our staff.

Contest. By dangling a Grand Prize much bigger than any we'd ever offered before (more about that later), we felt we'd receive a great response.

We just didn't know we'd be overwhelmed.

More than *34,000 recipes* poured in from our readers in a little more than a month! This incredible response provided vivid evidence that our audience *loves* cookies.

The entries filled huge crates in our offices and required a host of assistants to open, screen and file by category. We also had to record the date each was received to assure giving proper credit in case of duplicates.

It was a gigantic task, yet it made us confident that— with over 34,000 family favorites to choose from—we were bound to come up with a really *special* cookie as the overall winner. What's more, by carefully selecting over 250 of the *best* recipes from among those 34,000 entries, we could produce this "Cookie Book of All Cookie Books".

Back to the Beginning

That's getting ahead of the story. Actually, this contest and this story began last year, when our company— Reiman Publications—prepared to open its brand-new Visitor Center in downtown Greendale.

Our goal was to have this Center clearly convey the warmth and friendliness that subscribers say they find in our company's magazines. We wanted visitors to sense that same feeling as soon as they walked in the door.

After some discussion, we decided—with the Center's large test kitchen and our strong emphasis on food in our magazines—what better way to convey that feeling than

WELCOME TO GREENDALE. Flower beds and hanging baskets add color to historic village's main street, where Visitor Center is located.

HERE IT IS, our brand-new Visitor Center on main street.

to have visitors immediately note the unmatchable aroma of freshly baked cookies?

And that's when the idea for the "Cookie of All Cookies" contest originated. This could offer us the opportunity for those "just-out-of-the-oven" cookies to greet visitors…and then they would be asked to participate in the "judging".

That's the way the contest was conducted. Each day, a half dozen or so cookie recipes from readers were tested and offered to visitors at a modest price (all sales proceeds have been contributed to benefit Greendale community projects).

Each taster was asked to fill out a small "Cookie Judge's Rating Sheet" to tell us which cookie she or he liked best. This daily reaction was tallied by the test kitchen staff to determine the finalists.

This testing was done slowly and meticulously; visitors were often personally interviewed and asked the reason they preferred this cookie or that. Our food staff gauged the percentage of people who objected to raisins in a cookie, how many didn't like nuts in them, etc.

There was good reason for this detail: "If we're ♂

HERE COME THE JUDGES. Around 200 people per day stop in at our company Visitor Center, some arriving in groups by motorcoach as shown above. We recommend that groups call first (1-414/423-3080) so we'll be ready for you. At right, a group is watching our kitchen crew at work before getting to judge a fresh batch of cookies.

Best of Country Cookies

going to search for the 'Cookie of All Cookies', it has to be a really *outstanding* cookie," our publisher said when we began the contest. "Just as Mrs. Fields has her cookie, and Famous Amos has his, we'll be looking for the '*Taste of Home* Cookie'. We want to make this cookie just as famous as theirs. Frankly, we'd like ours to be even *better* than theirs."

And that's what we set out to do. The process took nearly a year…screening, filing, testing, tasting, retesting. There are four ovens in the Visitor Center's modern test kitchen, and at times they were all turning out different cookies, from drop cookies to sandwich cookies and from brownies to cutouts.

Finally, after testing *hundreds* of recipes and baking *thousands* of tasty morsels, our food staff—basing much of their judgment on what they'd learned from nearly 7,000 "subscriber-tasters"—carefully singled out the "top 14" recipes.

Then, after a good deal of debate and even more retesting of these 14 finalists, they came to a group consensus and…ta-daa…selected the "Cookie of All Cookies"!

The Envelope, Please…

The Grand Prize winner—the country cook whose recipe for "*Mmm*minnesota Munchers" was selected from over *34,000* entries—is Marcia Severson of Hallock, Minnesota, a tiny community of 1,300 in the northwest corner of that state, just 10 miles from the Canadian border. Congratulations, Marcia! You're the "Cookie Queen"!

But, before you start looking for it, let us point out that you won't find Marcia's recipe for her winning cookie in this book. Or anywhere else. You see, just as Mrs. Fields keeps her recipes secret, this one will be kept secret by the winner and Reiman Publications. It will not be published in any of our magazines nor offered for sale.

Instead of sharing the *recipe*,

"WILL YOU SIGN IN, PLEASE?" Visitors are asked to sign our guest book at the reception desk so we know where they're from.

BUSY BAKERS. Home economists Judy Scholovich and Betty Reuter keep ovens going at the Center's test kitchen. Note large mirror above them to help visitors observe process. At right, Anita Bukowski readies another batch for testing.

Introduction

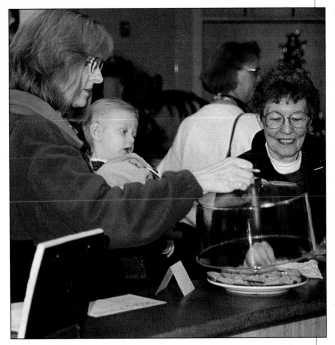

"HELLO, LET ME EXPLAIN how we go about our testing," says Judy Scholovich at the counter of our test kitchen. The kitchen's well equipped with four ovens, two microwaves, two large dishwashers, plenty of counter space...and lots of cookie jars! At left, Judy prepares to test one of the many recipes baked each day.

TESTING, TESTING. Visitors of all ages and from all states and Canada tasted, compared and then judged hundreds of cookies.

we'll share the *cookie*. It will be sold at our Visitor Center and, if present plans work out, through other outlets around the country. We're also looking into offering the "secret" ingredients by mail so you can bake a batch.

As a result, this winning recipe could result in a sizable income for Marcia, because, as promised at the outset of the contest, *she will receive a percentage of all the sales proceeds for as long as the cookie is sold.*

So while you won't find the recipe for the winner in this book, you *will* find the recipes for *277* "runners-up". And among those, you'll find the recipes for the 13 other "finalists" that came *so close* to winning.

When we announced this contest, we offered only a singular prize, the one for the winner. But we felt the other 13 who made the "finals" (see pages 14-17) deserved more than just congratulations. So, we've sent these 13 cooks

"I'D RATE THIS ONE NO. 1." Visitors tasted and compared, then indicated their opinion on "Judge's Rating Form" before inserting in tally box (at left). Our food staff also interviewed many tasters personally and asked reasons they preferred this cookie or that.

Editor. "After all, we had over 30,000 to pick from, so *every one* of those we carefully selected for this book is an absolutely out-of-this-world cookie."

Try a few of them and see for yourself. Keep in mind that each was already the tried-and-true family favorite of the country cook who shared it…so before long it's likely to become the same for your family as well.

Just Point Your Finger and Bake

Yes, you should be able to just point at any cookie in this book and then bake it with confidence. That's because we've already thoroughly screened out any so-so recipes.

We could have easily included 500 cookie recipes in this book. In a way, that would have been easier, because we wouldn't have had to go back and retest and retaste to cut the selection in half. But then we would have had to charge nearly twice as much for the book.

Better, we felt, that we do the tighter selection for you and others, thereby cutting the cost while delivering "the heart of the melon", the 277 *best* from *over 34,000*.

There…you're now holding the "Cookie Book of All Cookie Books". So browse, then bake. Predictably, when your family opens the door this evening, they're going to go *"Mmmm!"* as they enjoy the unmatchable just-out-of-the-oven aroma that greets subscribers as they walk into our company Visitor Center each day.

With that, happy baking…and come see us at the Center soon…so you can see what's cooking in our kitchen…and we can chat about what you've been cooking in yours.

who "nearly won" a free copy of our largest and most expensive hardcover cookbook, *The Complete Guide to Country Cooking*. In addition, we first had each one personally autographed by its editor, Mary Beth Jung.

As promised early on, we sent a free copy of this *Best of Country Cookies* book—as soon as it came off the press—to every one of the cooks whose cookie recipe is featured within these pages.

Speaking of the 250-plus recipes in this book, "We feel each is a *dynamite* recipe," says Coleen Martin, our Food

Introduction

AND FINALLY...staff members Ann Kaiser, Faithann Stoner and Mary Beth Jung (right), along with Food Editor Coleen Martin and other eager "helpers" in our offices, singled out the "top 14". After still more testing and discussion of these semifinalists, they agreed on the winner (shown below). Everyone agreed that it's absolutely *scrumptious*!

THE WINNER! From over *34,000* recipes, Marcia Severson's *"Mmm*minnesota Munchers" were chosen the Grand Prize winner. The recipe's tantalizing mix of chocolate chips, toffee bits and chopped pecans had subscriber-testers reaching for seconds and tagging it as simply "the best cookie they had ever tasted!"

Best of Country Cookies

TELL US WHERE YOU'RE FROM. Visitors eagerly put a pin to mark their hometown in the large map at the Center. To date, over 7,000 visitors—from every state, every province of Canada and at least nine foreign countries—have stopped in.

LET'S GET ACQUAINTED. At left, subscribers from across the country enjoy meeting and chatting while relaxing in the Center's lounge area.

Y'ALL COME! The friendly Visitor Center staffers at right are eager to meet even more of our subscribers. Behind them and on display at the Center is the famous custom-made wagon our company's six Belgian draft horses pulled across the country from Maine to California several years ago. *Over 50,000* people rode this wagon during that trip, and seeing it brings back fond memories for many of the visitors who were included in that group.

Introduction

THINK OF THIS PHOTO AS A "COOKIE SHEET". One of our photographers, Scott Anderson, came up with a *wonderful* idea as he was taking this picture of an assortment of the cookies tested for this book. "Let's print this photo on bed sheets for children's bedrooms," he said excitedly. "We'll call them 'Cookie Sheets'!" So, our Country Store crew is now working on that, and we'll hopefully be offering these colorful, one-of-a-kind sheets soon. Kids should love it—just imagine being able to take this many cookies to bed and Mom not saying a word about crumbs!

These Great Cookies

Here are a baker's dozen of fabulous finalists that were just one step away from being the overall winner. These recipes are identified on following pages with three cookie cutter "stars".

German Chocolate Toffee Cookies *(page 39)*
shared by Joyce Robb, Dillon, Montana

Tasters' Comments: "Tastes similar to chocolate cake"…"Chocolate flavor is subtle, not too sweet"… "German chocolate instead of semisweet chocolate makes it unique."

Oatmeal Crispies *(page 19)*
shared by Karen Henson, St. Louis, Missouri

Tasters' Comments: "This drop cookie has a hint of nutmeg"…"It's crispy outside, chewy inside"… "It's an improved version of a basic oatmeal cookie with nutmeg"…"It's *delicious!*"

Final Exam Brownies *(page 83)*
shared by Phyllis Crawford, Natrona Heights, Pa.

Tasters' Comments: "Moist and *very* chocolaty"… "Would definitely give you the energy to stay up studying"…"The miniature marshmallows make these brownies different from most other brownie recipes"…"These get a high grade with me!"

Nearly Won It All!

***Apricot Squares** (page 83)*
shared by Pat Ruggiero, Okemos, Michigan

Tasters' Comments: "The apricot, orange and lemon flavors blend together beautifully"…"Very rich and buttery"…"Well received by tasters at the Visitor Center, especially women"…"Great with coffee or tea!"

***Butter Pecan Cookies** (page 61)*
shared by Martha Thefield, Cedartown, Georgia

Tasters' Comments: "This cookie is true to its name"…"It especially appeals to adults"…"Very rich, buttery flavor, great for pecan lovers"…"Perfect cookie to represent the South."

***Quick Chocolate Sandwich Cookies** (page 109)*
shared by Mary Rempel, Altona, Manitoba

Tasters' Comments: "Most sandwich cookies take some time to prepare, but these get a head start with a cake mix"…"Young and old alike seemed to love these"…"These large, thick cookies are a delicious mouthful!"

7 More Finalists on Next 2 Pages

Double Butterscotch Cookies *(page 91)*
shared by Beverly Duncan, Big Prairie, Ohio

Tasters' Comments: "One of the *very best* butter-scotch cookies ever"…"Slices nicely, makes large cookies"…"Loaded with toffee bits and pecans"… "The 'double butterscotch' comes from the brown sugar and toffee bits."

Five-Chip Cookies *(page 33)*
shared by Sharon Hedstrom, Minnetonka, Minnesota

Tasters' Comments: "One of the most outstanding cookies tested; caught everyone's attention"…"These cookies are chewy with lots of flavor in every bite"… "With peanut butter and five kinds of chips, who *wouldn't* like a cookie like this?"

Small cookie cutter "stars" like these identify recipes of these near-winners on following pages.

White Chocolate Macadamia Cookies *(p. 25)*
shared by Mrs. Eddie Lennon, Newport, Tennessee

Tasters' Comments: "No wonder this is her family's favorite cookie"…"The vanilla chips and maca-damia nuts are a wonderfully different combina-tion"…"Rich, buttery morsels are a nice change of pace from chocolate chip cookies."

Caramel Creams *(page 97)*
shared by Barbara Youngers, Kingman, Kansas

Tasters' Comments: "These got four stars out of a possible five with us"…"You can make these sandwich cookies 'plain', but the brown butter filling really provides the icing on the cake!"

Double Chocolate Sprinkle Cookies *(page 103)*
shared by Barb Meinholz, South Milwaukee, Wisconsin

Tasters' Comments: "There wasn't anyone who *didn't* like these cookies; they appeal to all"…"The chocolate sprinkles help make this cookie unique"… "With the chocolate chips and sprinkles, these chewy cookies are simply *delicious*."

Cherry Almond Chews *(page 39)*
shared by Alma Chaney, Trenton, Ohio

Tasters' Comments: "They're tender, slightly sweet and delicious"…"Everyone loves these cookies at the Visitor Center"…"Especially nice-looking cookie for Christmas"…"These should freeze well."

Fruit 'n' Spice Rounds *(page 45)*
shared by Allison Bell, Helena, Montana

Tasters' Comments: "The lemon glaze adds a nice touch"…"These are hearty cookies"…"They not only taste great, they look great"…"These remind me of good old-fashioned cookies"…"Dates, raisins, walnuts…*mmm!*"

Raisin Chocolate Chip Cookies

Carol Jernigan, Everett, Washington

One day when making cookies, I discovered I didn't have any eggs. In a panic, I called my grandmother for expert advice, and she told me to use mayonnaise. These turned out to be the most moist and delicious cookies I'd ever eaten!

    1 cup raisins
    1 cup butter *or* margarine, softened
  3/4 cup sugar
  3/4 cup packed brown sugar
  1/4 cup mayonnaise*
    1 teaspoon vanilla extract
2-1/4 cups all-purpose flour
    1 teaspoon salt
    1 teaspoon baking soda
    1 cup (6 ounces) semisweet chocolate chips
  1/2 cup chopped walnuts

Place raisins in a bowl. Cover with boiling water; let stand for 5 minutes. Drain well and set aside. In a mixing bowl, cream butter and sugars. Beat in mayonnaise and vanilla. Combine flour, salt and baking soda; gradually add to the creamed mixture. Stir in the chocolate chips, walnuts and raisins. Drop by level tablespoonfuls 2 in. apart onto ungreased baking sheets. Bake at 375° for 9-11 minutes or until golden brown. Remove to wire racks to cool. **Yield:** about 7 dozen. ***Editor's Note:** Light or fat-free mayonnaise may not be substituted for regular mayonnaise.

Strawberry Pecan Cookies

Bonnie Black, North Olmsted, Ohio

My dad's wife is always creating new recipes to use up the fruits and vegetables he grows in his garden. These cake-like cookies are one of her "masterpieces"!

    1 cup shortening
1-1/2 cups sugar
    2 eggs
  3/4 cup strawberry puree (about 7 large
        strawberries)
    3 cups all-purpose flour
    1 teaspoon salt
  1/2 teaspoon baking soda
  3/4 cup chopped pecans
Red food coloring, optional

In a mixing bowl, cream shortening and sugar. Add eggs, one at a time, beating well after each addition. Beat in puree just until blended. Combine flour, salt

and baking soda; gradually add to the creamed mixture. Stir in pecans and food coloring if desired. Drop by tablespoonfuls 2 in. apart onto greased baking sheets. Bake at 350° for 12-15 minutes or until edges are lightly browned. Remove to wire racks to cool. **Yield:** about 6-1/2 dozen.

Swedish Oatmeal Drops

Anne Kluza, Baltimore, Maryland

A cousin of mine from Sweden shared this recipe while working as a cook in the U.S. I like these cookies because they adapt well to whatever nuts I have on hand.

    1 cup butter (no substitutes), melted
    1 cup quick-cooking oats
    1 egg
    1 cup sugar
    1 teaspoon vanilla extract
    1 cup all-purpose flour
    1 cup flaked coconut
    1 cup chopped nuts
    1 teaspoon baking powder

In a large bowl, pour butter over oats. Stir to coat; let stand for 10 minutes. In a small bowl, combine the egg, sugar and vanilla; pour over oat mixture. Combine flour, coconut, nuts and baking powder; gradually add to the oat mixture. Drop by rounded teaspoonfuls 2 in. apart onto ungreased baking sheets. Bake at 350° for 9-11 minutes or until edges are golden brown. Cool for 5 minutes before removing to wire racks. **Yield:** 5-1/2 dozen.

Tutti-Frutti Favorites

Joyce Robbins, Old Hickory, Tennessee

Of the recipes I've collected through the years, this one's most requested by family and friends. Packed with raisins, cornflakes and dried fruit, these hearty cookies are both delicious and nutritious.

  3/4 cup butter-flavored shortening
    1 cup sugar
  1/2 cup molasses
  1/4 cup honey
    2 eggs
    2 cups all-purpose flour
    2 cups quick-cooking oats
    1 teaspoon baking soda
    1 teaspoon salt
    1 teaspoon ground cinnamon
2-1/2 cups cornflakes

1 cup chopped mixed dried fruit
3/4 cup raisins

In a mixing bowl, cream shortening and sugar. Beat in molasses and honey. Add the eggs, one at a time, beating well after each addition. Combine flour, oats, baking soda, salt and cinnamon; gradually add to the creamed mixture. Stir in cornflakes, dried fruit and raisins. Drop by teaspoonfuls 2 in. apart onto ungreased baking sheets. Bake at 350° for 14-16 minutes or until the edges are firm. Remove to wire racks to cool. **Yield:** 9 dozen.

Marbled Chocolate Peanut Cookies

Shirley De Lange, Byron Center, Michigan

This recipe came about by accident when I was making both my husband's favorite peanut butter cookies and my favorite chocolate cookies. I had two small portions of dough left over and decided to combine them into one flavor-filled cookie.

PEANUT BUTTER DOUGH:
    1 cup butter (no substitutes), softened
    1 cup peanut butter
1-1/4 cups sugar
1-1/4 cups packed brown sugar
    3 eggs
    2 teaspoons vanilla extract
2-1/2 cups all-purpose flour
    1/2 teaspoon baking soda
    1/2 teaspoon salt
    1 cup chopped peanuts
CHOCOLATE DOUGH:
    1 cup butter (no substitutes), softened
    1 cup packed brown sugar
    3/4 cup sugar
    3 eggs
    2 teaspoons vanilla extract
2-1/2 cups all-purpose flour
    1/2 cup baking cocoa
    1/2 teaspoon baking soda
    1/2 teaspoon salt
    2 cups (12 ounces) semisweet chocolate chips

In a mixing bowl, cream butter, peanut butter and sugars. Add eggs, one at a time, beating well after each addition. Beat in vanilla. Combine flour, baking soda and salt; gradually add to the creamed mixture. Stir in peanuts; set aside. For chocolate dough, cream butter and sugars in another mixing bowl. Add eggs, one at a time, beating well after each addition. Beat in vanilla. Combine flour, cocoa, baking soda and salt; gradually add to the creamed mixture. Stir in chocolate chips. Gently fold in peanut butter dough until slightly marbled. Drop by heaping tablespoonfuls 3 in. apart onto greased baking sheets. Bake at 350°

for 14-16 minutes or until lightly browned and firm. Remove to wire racks to cool. **Yield:** 9-1/2 dozen.

Tea Cakes

Doris McGough, Dothan, Alabama

I've baked many batches of different cookies through the years, but family and friends tell me these are the best. The simple buttery flavor appeals to all.

    1 cup butter (no substitutes), softened
1-1/2 cups sugar
    3 eggs
    1 tablespoon vanilla extract
    3 cups all-purpose flour
    1 tablespoon baking powder
    1/4 teaspoon salt

In a mixing bowl, cream butter and sugar. Add eggs, one at a time, beating well after each addition. Beat in vanilla. Combine flour, baking powder and salt; gradually add to the creamed mixture (the dough will be soft). Drop by teaspoonfuls 2 in. apart onto greased baking sheets. Bake at 375° for 7-8 minutes or until the edges are golden brown. Remove to wire racks to cool. **Yield:** 9 dozen.

Nutty Sugar Crisps

Eleanore Kovach, Lakeview, Oregon

With chopped walnuts, these slightly crisp cookies are a little different than traditional sugar cookies. This recipe is especially appealing to folks who don't want the hassle of cutout cookies.

    1 cup butter *or* margarine, softened
    1/2 cup vegetable oil
    1 cup sugar
    1 cup confectioners' sugar
    2 eggs
    1 teaspoon vanilla extract
4-1/2 cups all-purpose flour
    1 teaspoon baking soda
    1 teaspoon cream of tartar
    1 cup chopped walnuts

In a mixing bowl, cream butter, oil and sugars. Add eggs, one at a time, beating well after each addition. Beat in vanilla. Combine the flour, baking soda and cream of tartar; gradually add to the creamed mixture. Stir in walnuts. Drop by teaspoonfuls 2 in. apart onto ungreased baking sheets. Flatten slightly with a glass dipped in sugar. Bake at 375° for 10-12 minutes or until edges are golden brown. Remove to wire racks to cool. **Yield:** 8-1/2 dozen.

Cranberry Crisps

Sandy Furches, Lake City, Florida

I developed this recipe after sampling a similar cookie while traveling in North Carolina. These pretty cookies keep well in the freezer, so I always have some on hand for midday munching.

- 1 cup butter-flavored shortening
- 1 cup sugar
- 1 cup packed brown sugar
- 2 eggs
- 2 teaspoons vanilla extract
- 2-1/2 cups old-fashioned oats
- 2 cups all-purpose flour
- 1 teaspoon baking soda
- 1 teaspoon ground cinnamon
- 1/2 teaspoon salt
- 1/2 teaspoon baking powder
- 1-1/3 cups dried cranberries
- 1 cup coarsely chopped walnuts

In a mixing bowl, cream shortening and sugars. Add eggs, one at a time, beating well after each addition. Beat in vanilla. Combine oats, flour, baking soda, cinnamon, salt and baking powder; gradually add to the creamed mixture. Stir in the cranberries and walnuts. Drop by tablespoonfuls 2 in. apart onto lightly greased baking sheets. Bake at 350° for 12-14 minutes or until lightly browned. Remove to wire racks to cool. **Yield:** 5 dozen.

Pecan Spice Drops

Donna Ann Wood, Goodman, Mississippi

I was thrilled when a dear friend shared her grandmother's spice cookie recipe with me. She assured me I would love them…and she was right!

- 1 cup butter *or* margarine, melted
- 2 cups sugar
- 2 eggs
- 1 teaspoon vanilla extract
- 3 cups all-purpose flour
- 1 teaspoon baking soda
- 1 teaspoon *each* ground cinnamon, nutmeg, allspice and cloves
- 1/2 teaspoon salt
- 2 cups chopped pecans

In a mixing bowl, combine butter and sugar. Add the eggs, one at a time, beating well after each addition. Beat in vanilla. Combine flour, baking soda, spices and salt; gradually add to the creamed mixture.

Stir in pecans. Drop by tablespoonfuls 2 in. apart onto ungreased baking sheets. Bake at 350° for 12-14 minutes or until edges are firm. Remove to wire racks to cool. **Yield:** 4-1/2 dozen.

Toffee Chip Thins

Lynae Lang, Wolf Point, Montana

In an attempt to create the "ultimate" cookie, I took the best features from my favorite recipes to create this sweet, crisp cookie. My family can't get enough of them.

- 1/2 cup butter *or* margarine, softened
- 1 can (14 ounces) sweetened condensed milk
- 2 cups graham cracker crumbs (about 32 squares)
- 3/4 cup all-purpose flour
- 2 teaspoons baking powder
- 2 cups (12 ounces) semisweet chocolate chips
- 1 cup English toffee bits *or* almond brickle chips
- 1-1/2 cups flaked coconut, optional

In a mixing bowl, combine butter and condensed milk; mix well. Combine cracker crumbs, flour and baking powder; gradually add to the butter mixture. Stir in chocolate chips, toffee bits and coconut if desired. Drop by rounded tablespoonfuls 2 in. apart onto greased baking sheets. Bake at 375° for 10-12 minutes or until edges are lightly browned. Cool for 2 minutes before removing to wire racks. **Yield:** about 4-1/2 dozen.

Frosted Zucchini Cookies

Michele Bretz-Hysong, Massillon, Ohio

Friends and family gladly share garden-fresh zucchini with me so I can make and give away many batches of these cookies. I keep shredded zucchini in the freezer so we can enjoy them in winter as well. A cream cheese frosting makes them especially delicious.

- 1/2 cup butter *or* margarine, softened
- 1 cup sugar
- 1 egg
- 2 cups all-purpose flour
- 1 teaspoon baking soda
- 1 teaspoon ground cinnamon
- 1/2 teaspoon salt
- 1/4 to 1/2 teaspoon ground cloves, optional
- 1 cup finely shredded zucchini
- 1 cup raisins
- 1 cup chopped walnuts

FROSTING:
- 1/4 cup butter *or* margarine, softened
- 1 package (3 ounces) cream cheese, softened
- 1 teaspoon vanilla extract
- 2 cups confectioners' sugar

In a mixing bowl, cream butter and sugar. Beat in egg. Combine the flour, baking soda, cinnamon, salt and cloves if desired; add to creamed mixture alternately with zucchini. Stir in raisins and walnuts. Cover and refrigerate for 2 hours. Drop by heaping teaspoonfuls 2 in. apart onto lightly greased baking sheets. Bake at 375° for 12-15 minutes or until lightly browned. Remove to wire racks. In a small mixing bowl, cream butter, cream cheese and vanilla. Gradually beat in confectioners' sugar. Frost the cooled cookies. **Yield:** about 5 dozen.

Date Macaroons

Jessie Bethune, Trion, Georgia

This recipe from my sister originally made a pie. But I decided to turn it into a cookie with mouth-watering results. They're so easy to make and very tasty.

- 1 cup sugar
- 1/4 cup finely crushed saltines (about 15 crackers)
- 1/2 teaspoon baking powder
- 1-1/3 cups flaked coconut
- 3/4 cup chopped pecans
- 1/2 cup chopped dates
- 1 teaspoon vanilla extract
- 3 egg whites

In a large bowl, combine sugar, cracker crumbs and baking powder; stir in coconut, pecans, dates and vanilla. In a small mixing bowl, beat egg whites until stiff peaks form; fold into coconut mixture. Drop by tablespoonfuls 2 in. apart onto lightly greased baking sheets. Bake at 300° for 12-14 minutes or until edges are lightly browned. Cool for 2 minutes before removing to wire racks. **Yield:** 3-1/2 dozen.

Molasses Raisin Chews

Barbara Parker, Middlefield, Connecticut

When I was a child, we always looked forward to visiting my aunt's farm. As soon as we arrived, she'd offer a plate of these chewy treats. We called them "Cry Baby Cookies" because we thought the three raisins on each one resembled two eyes and an open mouth.

- 1/2 cup shortening
- 1 cup sugar

- 1 cup molasses
- 4 cups all-purpose flour
- 2 teaspoons baking soda
- 2 teaspoons ground cinnamon
- 1 teaspoon ground cloves
- 1/4 teaspoon salt
- 1 cup milk
- 1 cup raisins

In a mixing bowl, cream shortening and sugar. Beat in molasses. Combine flour, baking soda, cinnamon, cloves and salt; add to the creamed mixture alternately with milk. Drop by heaping tablespoonfuls 2 in. apart onto greased baking sheets. Arrange three raisins on each cookie. Bake at 350° for 10-12 minutes or until set. Remove to wire racks to cool. **Yield:** about 5-1/2 dozen.

Oat-rageous Cookies

Dianne Birchler, Brookston, Indiana

I simply love oatmeal cookies. I've added a variety of different goodies to the batter and think this combination is by far the best. It's especially tasty in autumn.

- 1/2 cup shortening
- 1/2 cup sugar
- 1/2 cup packed brown sugar
- 1 egg
- 1 tablespoon water
- 1/2 teaspoon vanilla extract
- 1 cup all-purpose flour
- 1/2 teaspoon baking soda
- 1/2 teaspoon salt
- 1 cup quick-cooking oats
- 1 cup (6 ounces) semisweet chocolate chips
- 3/4 cup dried cranberries
- 1/2 cup chopped walnuts
- 1/2 cup English toffee bits *or* almond brickle chips

In a mixing bowl, cream shortening and sugars. Beat in egg, water and vanilla. Combine flour, baking soda and salt; gradually add to the creamed mixture. Stir in remaining ingredients. Drop by tablespoonfuls 3 in. apart onto ungreased baking sheets. Bake at 375° for 10-12 minutes or until lightly browned. Cool for 2 minutes before removing to wire racks. **Yield:** 4-1/2 dozen.

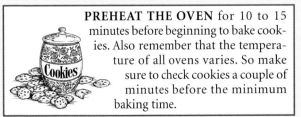

PREHEAT THE OVEN for 10 to 15 minutes before beginning to bake cookies. Also remember that the temperature of all ovens varies. So make sure to check cookies a couple of minutes before the minimum baking time.

Double Chocolate Crisps

Marilyn Spangler, Oak Creek, Wisconsin

(Pictured at left)

I received this recipe from my sister-in-law more than 35 years ago. Chock-full of chocolate, these crispy cookies have a tantalizing aroma while baking.

   1 cup butter (no substitutes), softened
   2 cups sugar
   2 eggs
   4 squares (1 ounce *each*) unsweetened
      chocolate, melted and cooled
   2 teaspoons vanilla extract
2-1/4 cups all-purpose flour
   1 teaspoon baking soda
   1 teaspoon salt
1/4 teaspoon ground cinnamon
   1 cup (6 ounces) semisweet chocolate chips
   1 cup chopped pecans

In a mixing bowl, cream butter and sugar. Add eggs, one at time, beating well after each addition. Beat in chocolate and vanilla. Combine the flour, baking soda, salt and cinnamon; gradually add to the creamed mixture. Stir in chocolate chips and pecans. Drop by tablespoonfuls 2 in. apart onto ungreased baking sheets. Bake at 375° for 10-12 minutes or until tops are cracked. Remove to wire racks to cool. **Yield:** 4 dozen.

Toffee Almond Sandies

Vicki Crowley, Monticello, Iowa

(Pictured at left)

I knew after sampling these cookies from a friend that I had to add the recipe to my bulging files!

   1 cup butter *or* margarine, softened
   1 cup vegetable oil
   1 cup sugar
   1 cup confectioners' sugar
   2 eggs
   1 teaspoon almond extract
4-1/2 cups all-purpose flour
   1 teaspoon baking soda
   1 teaspoon cream of tartar
   1 teaspoon salt
   2 cups sliced almonds

NUT-FILLED FAVORITES. Pictured at left, top to bottom: Double Chocolate Crisps, Toffee Almond Sandies and White Chocolate Macadamia Cookies (all recipes on this page).

---

   1 package English toffee bits (10 ounces) *or* almond brickle chips (7-1/2 ounces)

In a mixing bowl, cream butter, oil and sugars. Add eggs, one at a time, beating well after each addition. Beat in extract. Combine flour, baking soda, cream of tartar and salt; gradually add to the creamed mixture. Stir in almonds and toffee bits. Drop by teaspoonfuls 2 in. apart onto ungreased baking sheets. Bake at 350° for 10-12 minutes or until golden brown. Remove to wire racks to cool. **Yield:** 9 dozen.

White Chocolate Macadamia Cookies

Mrs. Eddie Lennon, Newport, Tennessee

(Pictured at left)

Vanilla chips and macadamia nuts are a delightful duo in these rich, buttery morsels. They are a nice change from chocolate chip cookies.

1/2 cup butter *or* margarine, softened
2/3 cup sugar
   1 egg
   1 teaspoon vanilla extract
   1 cup plus 2 tablespoons all-purpose flour
1/2 teaspoon baking soda
   1 jar (3-1/2 ounces) macadamia nuts, chopped
   1 cup vanilla chips

In a mixing bowl, cream butter and sugar. Beat in the egg and vanilla. Combine flour and baking soda; gradually add to creamed mixture. Stir in nuts and vanilla chips. Drop by heaping teaspoonfuls 2 in. apart onto ungreased baking sheets. Bake at 350° for 10-12 minutes or until golden brown. Cool for 1 minute before removing to wire racks. **Yield:** about 4-1/2 dozen.

Sunflower Cookies

Donna Cline, Pensacola, Florida

These cookies are a tradition in my Kansas hometown. Sometimes I add chopped nuts, raisins or dates.

1/2 cup vegetable oil
1/2 cup honey
   2 eggs
   1 teaspoon vanilla extract
1-1/2 cups whole wheat flour
   1 cup sunflower kernels
1/4 teaspoon salt

In a large bowl, combine the oil, honey, eggs and vanilla. Add the remaining ingredients; mix well (dough will be very soft). Drop by heaping teaspoonfuls 2 in. apart onto greased baking sheets. Bake at 350° for 10-12 minutes or until golden brown. Remove to wire racks to cool. **Yield:** 4 dozen.

Soft Ginger Puffs

Marion Lowery, Medford, Oregon

These spice cookies loaded with raisins and walnuts really do appeal to all generations—I found the recipe in a 1901 South Dakota cookbook! Sour cream adds a wonderful, unusual flair.

- 1/2 cup butter *or* margarine, softened
- 3/4 cup sugar
- 3 eggs
- 1 cup molasses
- 1 cup (8 ounces) sour cream
- 3-1/2 cups all-purpose flour
- 2 teaspoons ground ginger
- 1 teaspoon baking soda
- 1/2 teaspoon *each* ground allspice, cinnamon and nutmeg
- 1-1/2 cups raisins
- 1-1/2 cups chopped walnuts

In a mixing bowl, cream butter and sugar. Add eggs, one at a time, beating well after each addition. Beat in molasses and sour cream. Combine flour, ginger, baking soda, allspice, cinnamon and nutmeg; gradually add to the creamed mixture. Stir in raisins and walnuts. Drop by tablespoonfuls 1 in. apart onto greased baking sheets. Bake at 375° for 10-12 minutes or until the edges begin to brown. Remove to wire racks to cool. **Yield:** 8 dozen.

Chocolate Zucchini Cookies

Tina Lunt, Bass Harbor, Maine

This recipe started out as a plain zucchini cookie. But over the years, I added nuts and chocolate chips. These soft cookies never make it to the cookie jar!

- 1 cup butter *or* margarine, softened
- 2 cups sugar
- 2 eggs
- 4 cups all-purpose flour
- 2 teaspoons baking soda
- 2 teaspoons ground cinnamon
- 1 teaspoon salt
- 1 teaspoon ground nutmeg
- 1 teaspoon ground cloves
- 2 cups finely shredded zucchini
- 1 cup chopped nuts
- 1/2 cup semisweet chocolate chips

In a mixing bowl, cream butter and sugar. Add the eggs, one at a time, beating well after each addition. Combine the flour, baking soda, cinnamon, salt, nut-

meg and cloves; gradually add to the creamed mixture. Stir in the zucchini, nuts and chocolate chips. Drop by tablespoonfuls 3 in. apart onto ungreased baking sheets. Bake at 375° for 10-12 minutes or until lightly browned. Remove to wire racks to cool. **Yield:** 8 dozen.

Oat-Bran Chocolate Chip Cookies

Judy Bergman, Helendale, California

While dabbling in the kitchen one day, my husband, Dale, came up with these hearty cookies. I begged him to make them again, but he hadn't written down the recipe. Ten batches later, he finally recaptured the wonderful flavor.

- 1 cup butter *or* margarine, softened
- 3/4 cup sugar
- 3/4 cup packed brown sugar
- 2 eggs
- 1 teaspoon vanilla extract
- 1-1/2 cups all-purpose flour
- 1 teaspoon baking soda
- 1 teaspoon salt
- 2-1/2 cups quick-cooking oats
- 1 package (11-1/2 ounces) milk chocolate chips
- 2 cups chopped walnuts
- 1-1/2 cups All-Bran cereal

In a mixing bowl, cream butter and sugars. Add the eggs, one at a time, beating well after each addition. Beat in vanilla. Combine the flour, baking soda and salt; gradually add to creamed mixture. Stir in the remaining ingredients. Drop by tablespoonfuls 2 in. apart onto ungreased baking sheets. Bake at 350° for 12-14 minutes or until lightly browned. Remove to wire racks to cool. **Yield:** 7 dozen.

Spiced Oatmeal Raisin Drops

Patsy Clark, Union, Ohio

My husband's two favorite snacks are oatmeal cookies and pumpkin pie. So in an effort to combine those flavors into one treat, I created this recipe.

- 1/2 cup butter *or* margarine, softened
- 1/2 cup shortening
- 1 cup packed brown sugar
- 1/2 cup sugar
- 2 eggs
- 1 teaspoon vanilla extract
- 3 cups quick-cooking oats
- 2 cups all-purpose flour

1-1/2 teaspoons pumpkin pie spice
1 teaspoon baking soda
1/2 teaspoon salt
1 cup raisins

In a mixing bowl, cream butter, shortening and sugars. Add eggs, one at a time, beating well after each addition. Beat in vanilla. Combine oats, flour, pumpkin pie spice, baking soda and salt; gradually add to the creamed mixture. Stir in raisins. Drop by rounded tablespoonfuls 2 in. apart onto ungreased baking sheets. Bake at 350° for 10-12 minutes or until lightly browned. Remove to wire racks to cool. **Yield:** 4-1/2 dozen.

Chewy Chocolate Chip Cookies

Iona Hamilton, Rocky Ford, Colorado

Everyone who has tried these cookies says they're the best they've ever eaten. I'm sure the addition of pudding mix makes all the difference.

1 cup butter *or* margarine, softened
3/4 cup packed brown sugar
1/4 cup sugar
1 package (3.4 ounces) instant vanilla pudding mix*
2 eggs
1 teaspoon vanilla extract
2-1/4 cups all-purpose flour
1 teaspoon baking soda
2 cups (12 ounces) semisweet chocolate chips
1 cup finely chopped walnuts

In a mixing bowl, cream butter, sugars and pudding mix. Add eggs, one at a time, beating well after each addition. Beat in vanilla. Combine flour and baking soda; gradually add to the creamed mixture. Stir in chocolate chips and walnuts (dough will be stiff). Drop by rounded teaspoonfuls 2 in. apart onto ungreased baking sheets. Bake at 350° for 8-10 minutes or until lightly browned. Remove to wire racks to cool. **Yield:** 9-1/2 dozen. ***Editor's Note:** One 3.9-ounce package of instant chocolate pudding mix may be substituted for the vanilla pudding mix.

Pecan Sandies

Jeanie Hanna, Rustburg, Virginia

My family prefers these pecan cookies to any store-bought variety. Self-rising flour makes them a little different from most cookie recipes.

1/3 cup butter *or* margarine, softened
1/3 cup shortening
1/2 cup sugar
1/2 cup packed brown sugar
1 egg
1 teaspoon vanilla extract
1-1/2 cups self-rising flour*
1/2 cup chopped pecans

In a mixing bowl, cream the butter, shortening and sugars. Beat in egg and vanilla. Gradually add flour. Stir in pecans. Drop by rounded teaspoonfuls 2 in. apart onto ungreased baking sheets. Bake at 375° for 9-11 minutes or until edges are lightly browned. Cool for 1-2 minutes before removing to wire racks. **Yield:** about 3-1/2 dozen. ***Editor's Note:** As a substitute for 1 cup self-rising flour, place 1-1/2 teaspoons baking powder and 1/2 teaspoon salt in a measuring cup; add all-purpose flour to measure 1 cup. For 1/2 cup self-rising flour, place 3/4 teaspoon baking powder and 1/4 teaspoon salt in a measuring cup; add all-purpose flour to measure 1/2 cup.

Toffee Cashew Treasures

Denise Sokolowski, Milwaukee, Wisconsin

After searching for a recipe that combined all of my favorite cookie ingredients, I decided to create my own. The result is a lacy, crisp cookie that's sure to earn you rave reviews.

1 cup butter (no substitutes), softened
1 cup sugar
1 cup packed brown sugar
2 eggs
1 teaspoon vanilla extract
2 cups all-purpose flour
2 cups old-fashioned oats
1 teaspoon baking soda
1/2 teaspoon baking powder
1/2 teaspoon salt
1 cup flaked coconut
1 cup English toffee bits *or* almond brickle chips
1 cup chopped cashews, toasted

In a mixing bowl, cream butter and sugars. Add the eggs, one at a time, beating well after each addition. Beat in vanilla. Combine flour, oats, baking soda, baking powder and salt; gradually add to the creamed mixture. Stir in the remaining ingredients. Cover and refrigerate for 6 hours or until easy to handle. Drop by rounded tablespoonfuls 3 in. apart onto ungreased baking sheets. Bake at 350° for 12-14 minutes or until lightly browned. Cool for 2 minutes before removing to wire racks. **Yield:** about 5 dozen.

Chewy Oatmeal Cookies

Ruth O'Donnell, Romeo, Michigan

When our family gathered at my aunt's summer home on Mackinac Island a few years back, she pulled out her tried-and-true recipe and made these wholesome cookies. I think of her and that memorable vacation every time I make these for my own family.

    1 cup butter *or* margarine, softened
    1 cup sugar
    1 cup packed brown sugar
    2 eggs
    1 teaspoon vanilla extract
1-1/2 cups all-purpose flour
    1 teaspoon baking soda
    1 teaspoon baking powder
    1 teaspoon salt
    2 cups quick-cooking oats
    2 cups cornflakes
    1 cup flaked coconut
    1 cup salted peanuts

In a mixing bowl, cream butter and sugars. Add the eggs, one at a time, beating well after each addition. Beat in vanilla. Combine flour, baking soda, baking powder and salt; gradually add to the creamed mixture. Stir in remaining ingredients. Drop by level tablespoonfuls 2 in. apart onto ungreased baking sheets. Bake at 350° for 10-12 minutes or until lightly browned. Remove to wire racks to cool. **Yield:** about 6-1/2 dozen.

Candied Cherry Hermits

Joy Townsend, Ponte Vedra Beach, Florida

Candied cherries give traditional spice hermit cookies a new taste twist. They're so moist and chewy it's hard to eat just one.

1/2 cup butter *or* margarine, softened
    1 cup packed brown sugar
    2 eggs
1-1/2 cups all-purpose flour
    1 to 2 teaspoons ground cinnamon
1/2 teaspoon baking soda
    1 cup chopped pecans
3/4 cup raisins, chopped
3/4 cup candied cherries, chopped

In a mixing bowl, cream butter and brown sugar. Add eggs, one at a time, beating well after each addition. Combine flour, cinnamon and baking soda; gradually add to the creamed mixture. Stir in pecans, raisins

and cherries. Drop by rounded tablespoonfuls 2 in. apart onto ungreased baking sheets. Bake at 375° for 10-12 minutes or until golden brown. Remove to wire racks to cool. **Yield:** about 3-1/2 dozen.

Soft Sugar Cookies

Karen Hoffer, Lititz, Pennsylvania

This recipe has been in the family for four generations. When I got married, Mom made sure to pass this recipe along. For variation, I sometimes eliminate the raisins and sprinkle the tops with colored sugar or leave them plain and frost when cooled.

    3/4 cup shortening
1-1/2 cups sugar
    2 eggs
    1 teaspoon vanilla extract
    3 cups all-purpose flour
    2 teaspoons baking powder
    1 teaspoon baking soda
1/2 teaspoon salt
    1 cup buttermilk
Raisins

In a mixing bowl, cream shortening and sugar. Add eggs, one at a time, beating well after each addition. Beat in vanilla. Combine flour, baking powder, baking soda and salt; add to the creamed mixture alternately with buttermilk. Cover and refrigerate for at least 2 hours (the dough will be very soft). Drop by tablespoonfuls 2 in. apart onto ungreased baking sheets. Place a raisin in the center of each cookie. Bake at 375° for 8-10 minutes or until lightly browned. Remove to wire racks to cool. **Yield:** about 6-1/2 dozen.

Frosted Raisin Creams

Kay Strain, Norwalk, Iowa

These old-fashioned raisin spice cookies bring back fond memories of Mom whipping up a batch in her kitchen. The down-home aroma as they bake is a wonderful way to welcome family home.

    1 cup raisins
1-1/4 cups boiling water
    1 cup butter *or* margarine, softened
1-1/2 cups sugar
    2 eggs
    3 cups all-purpose flour
    2 tablespoons ground cinnamon
    1 teaspoon baking soda
1/4 teaspoon salt

1/2 cup chopped walnuts
FROSTING:
    1/2 cup packed brown sugar
    1/2 cup hot milk
4-1/2 cups confectioners' sugar

Place raisins in a bowl. Add boiling water; let stand for 5 minutes. Drain, reserving 1 cup liquid; set the raisins and liquid aside. In a mixing bowl, cream butter and sugar. Add eggs, one at a time, beating well after each addition. Combine flour, cinnamon, baking soda and salt; add to the creamed mixture alternately with reserved liquid. Stir in walnuts and raisins. Drop by teaspoonfuls 2 in. apart onto ungreased baking sheets. Bake at 350° for 12-15 minutes or until lightly browned. Cool for 1 minute before removing to wire racks. For frosting, whisk brown sugar and milk until sugar is dissolved. Add confectioners' sugar; mix well. Frost cooled cookies. **Yield:** about 9 dozen.

Buttery Lace Cookies

Lillie Duhon, Port Neches, Texas

I worked with a group of engineers for over 30 years, and these cookies were a favorite of theirs. They go so well with a steaming cup of coffee or tea.

    2 cups quick-cooking oats
    2 cups sugar
    3 tablespoons all-purpose flour
1/2 teaspoon baking powder
    2 eggs
    1 teaspoon vanilla extract
    1 teaspoon lemon extract
1/4 teaspoon almond extract
    1 cup butter (no substitutes), melted
    1 cup chopped pecans

In a bowl, combine the first four ingredients. Add eggs, one at a time, beating well after each addition. Beat in extracts. Stir in butter and pecans. Drop by teaspoonfuls 3 in. apart onto lightly greased foil-lined baking sheets. Bake at 350° for 10-12 minutes or until lacy and golden brown. Cool completely on pans before carefully removing to wire racks. **Yield:** about 9 dozen.

Cranberry Nut Cookies

Machelle Wall, Rosamond, California

In fall, I stock up on fresh cranberries and freeze them so I can make these cookies throughout the year. Tangy cranberries are a nice addition to a buttery cookie.

2/3 cup butter *or* margarine, softened
    1 cup sugar
    1 cup packed brown sugar
    1 egg
1/4 cup milk
    2 tablespoons lemon juice
    3 cups all-purpose flour
1/4 cup ground walnuts
    1 teaspoon baking powder
1/2 teaspoon salt
1/4 teaspoon baking soda
2-1/2 cups halved fresh *or* frozen cranberries
    1 cup chopped walnuts

In a mixing bowl, cream butter and sugars. Beat in egg, milk and lemon juice. Combine flour, ground walnuts, baking powder, salt and baking soda; gradually add to the creamed mixture. Stir in the cranberries and chopped walnuts. Drop by heaping tablespoonfuls 2 in. apart onto lightly greased baking sheets. Bake at 350° for 16-18 minutes or until golden brown. Remove to wire racks to cool. **Yield:** 5 dozen.

Soft Orange Molasses Drops

Beverly Steiner, Mt. Cory, Ohio

Orange juice and peel add a slight citrus twist to ordinary molasses cookies. I've also stirred in some chopped nuts, raisins, prunes and apricots.

1/2 cup butter *or* margarine, softened
1/2 cup sugar
    1 egg
2-1/2 cups all-purpose flour
    1 teaspoon baking soda
    1 teaspoon ground ginger
1/2 teaspoon *each* ground cinnamon, cloves and nutmeg
1/2 cup molasses
1/4 cup orange juice
    2 teaspoons grated orange peel
GLAZE:
    1 cup confectioners' sugar
    1 to 2 tablespoons orange juice

In a mixing bowl, cream butter and sugar. Beat in egg. Combine flour, baking soda and spices; set aside. Combine molasses, orange juice and peel. Add dry ingredients to the creamed mixture alternately with the molasses mixture. Drop by tablespoonfuls 2 in. apart onto greased baking sheets. Bake at 375° for 10-12 minutes or until edges are set. Remove to wire racks. For glaze, combine confectioners' sugar and enough orange juice to achieve desired consistency. Spread over cooled cookies. **Yield:** 5 dozen.

Flatten with a glass dipped in sugar. Bake at 350° for 10-12 minutes or until edges are lightly browned. Remove to wire racks to cool. **Yield:** 5 dozen.

Crisp Peppermint Patties

Deborah Kay Collins, Mansfield, Ohio

Mint lovers will delight in every bite of these original crisp cookies. They not only taste wonderful, they're attractive as well.

- **1 cup butter-flavored shortening**
- **1/2 cup sugar**
- **1/2 cup packed brown sugar**
- **2 eggs**
- **1 package (13 ounces) chocolate-covered peppermint patties, melted**
- **1 teaspoon vanilla extract**
- **2-1/3 cups all-purpose flour**
- **1 teaspoon baking soda**
- **1/2 teaspoon salt**

In a mixing bowl, cream shortening and sugars. Add eggs, one at a time, beating well after each addition. Beat in melted peppermint patties and vanilla. Combine flour, baking soda and salt; gradually add to the creamed mixture. Cover and refrigerate for 30 minutes or until easy to handle. Drop by rounded teaspoonfuls 2 in. apart onto ungreased baking sheets. Bake at 375° for 8-10 minutes or until the surface cracks. Cool for 1-2 minutes before removing to wire racks. **Yield:** 5 dozen.

Banana Chip Cookies

JoAnne Wempe, Seneca, Kansas

While looking for a chocolate chip cookie that was a little different, I came up with this version. The result is a cake-like cookie that stands out from the rest. It's a great way to use up those ripe bananas.

- **3/4 cup shortening**
- **1 cup sugar**
- **2 eggs**
- **1/2 cup milk**
- **1/4 cup honey**
- **1 medium ripe banana, mashed**
- **4 cups all-purpose flour**
- **2 teaspoons baking powder**
- **1 teaspoon salt**
- **1 cup miniature semisweet chocolate chips**

In a mixing bowl, cream shortening and sugar. Add eggs, one at a time, beating well after each addition. Beat in milk, honey and banana. Combine flour, baking powder and salt; gradually add to the creamed mixture. Stir in chocolate chips. Drop by heaping teaspoonfuls 2 in. apart onto lightly greased baking sheets.

Pecan Surprises

Jean Ohnigian, Havertown, Pennsylvania

After I bought too many nuts for a different recipe, I decided to put the leftovers to use in a batch of cookies. Coconut and apricots add a little "surprise" to every bite.

- **1 cup butter *or* margarine, softened**
- **3/4 cup sugar**
- **3/4 cup packed brown sugar**
- **2 eggs**
- **1 teaspoon vanilla extract**
- **2 cups all-purpose flour**
- **3/4 cup ground pecans**
- **1 teaspoon baking soda**
- **1 teaspoon salt**
- **2 cups (12 ounces) semisweet chocolate chips**
- **2/3 cup flaked coconut**
- **2/3 cup finely chopped dried apricots**

In a mixing bowl, cream butter and sugars. Add the eggs, one at a time, beating well after each addition. Beat in vanilla. Combine flour, pecans, baking soda and salt; gradually add to the creamed mixture. Stir in remaining ingredients. Drop by tablespoonfuls 2 in. apart onto ungreased baking sheets. Bake at 375° for 10-12 minutes or until lightly browned. Cool for 1-2 minutes before removing to wire racks. **Yield:** 6 dozen.

Cherry Chocolate Nut Cookies

Sybil Noble, Hamburg, Arkansas

Each Christmas, I make about 600 cookies to share with family and friends. The holidays wouldn't be the same without several batches of these colorful goodies.

- **1/2 cup butter *or* margarine, softened**
- **1/2 cup sugar**
- **1/2 cup packed brown sugar**
- **1 egg**
- **1/4 cup milk**
- **1 teaspoon vanilla extract**
- **2 cups all-purpose flour**
- **1 teaspoon baking powder**
- **1/2 teaspoon salt**
- **1/4 teaspoon baking soda**
- **1 cup (6 ounces) semisweet chocolate chips**
- **3/4 cup chopped maraschino cherries**
- **3/4 cup chopped pecans**

In a mixing bowl, cream butter and sugars. Beat in egg, milk and vanilla. Combine flour, baking powder, salt and baking soda; gradually add to the creamed mixture. Stir in the remaining ingredients. Drop by tablespoonfuls 2 in. apart onto greased baking sheets. Bake at 375° for 10-12 minutes or until golden brown. Remove to wire racks to cool. **Yield:** 5 dozen.

Marmalade Chews

Shirleene Wilkins, Lake Placid, Florida

I live in the heart of citrus country and think this cookie really captures that area's flavor. Orange marmalade, juice and peel give the cookie and frosting a delightful tropical taste.

  1/4 cup shortening
  1/2 cup sugar
  1 egg
1-1/2 cups all-purpose flour
  1/4 teaspoon baking soda
  1/4 teaspoon salt
  1/2 cup orange marmalade
  1/2 cup chopped pecans, optional
FROSTING:
  2 cups confectioners' sugar
  2 tablespoons butter *or* margarine, melted
  1 teaspoon grated orange peel
  2 to 3 tablespoons orange juice

In a mixing bowl, cream shortening and sugar. Beat in egg. Combine flour, baking soda and salt; gradually add to the creamed mixture. Stir in marmalade and pecans if desired. Drop by heaping teaspoonfuls 2 in. apart onto greased baking sheets. Bake at 350° for 10-12 minutes or until golden brown. Remove to wire racks to cool. In a small mixing bowl, combine sugar, butter and orange peel. Add enough orange juice to achieve spreading consistency. Frost cooled cookies. **Yield:** about 4-1/2 dozen.

Frosted Chocolate Delights

Patricia Ramczyk, Appleton, Wisconsin

Before we five kids headed off to school each day, Mom took our requests for that day's dinner. I usually asked her to make these cookies for dessert, and she would rarely disappoint. I still enjoy them today.

  1/2 cup shortening
  1 cup packed brown sugar
  1 egg
  1/2 cup milk

  1 teaspoon vanilla extract
  2 squares (1 ounce *each*) unsweetened
    chocolate, melted
1-3/4 cups all-purpose flour
  1 teaspoon baking powder
  1/2 teaspoon salt
  1/4 teaspoon baking soda
  1/2 cup chopped walnuts
FROSTING:
  9 tablespoons butter *or* margarine, softened
4-1/2 cups confectioners' sugar
1-1/2 teaspoons vanilla extract
  6 to 8 tablespoons milk

In a mixing bowl, cream shortening and brown sugar. Beat in egg, milk and vanilla. Beat in chocolate until blended. Combine flour, baking powder, salt and baking soda; gradually add to the creamed mixture. Stir in walnuts. Drop by tablespoonfuls 2 in. apart onto ungreased baking sheets. Bake at 350° for 11-13 minutes or until firm. Remove to wire racks to cool. In a mixing bowl, cream butter and sugar. Beat in vanilla and enough milk to achieve spreading consistency. Frost cooled cookies. **Yield:** 5-1/2 dozen.

Golden Harvest Cookies

Florence Pope, Denver, Colorado

Folks may be skeptical when you tell them the ingredients in these cookies. But what a tantalizing treat for the taste buds! These unique cookies are just slightly sweet.

  2/3 cup butter *or* margarine, softened
  1/3 cup packed brown sugar
  1 egg
  1 teaspoon vanilla extract
  3/4 cup self-rising flour*
  1 teaspoon ground cinnamon
  1/8 teaspoon ground cloves
1-1/2 cups quick-cooking oats
  1 cup shredded carrots
  1 cup (4 ounces) shredded cheddar cheese
  1 cup chopped pecans
  1/2 cup raisins

In a mixing bowl, cream butter and brown sugar. Beat in egg and vanilla. Combine flour, cinnamon and cloves; gradually add to the creamed mixture. Stir in remaining ingredients. Drop by heaping tablespoonfuls 2 in. apart onto ungreased baking sheets. Bake at 375° for 12-14 minutes or until golden brown. Remove to wire racks to cool. Store in the refrigerator. **Yield:** 3-1/2 dozen. *Editor's Note: As a substitute for self-rising flour, place 1 teaspoon baking powder and 1/4 teaspoon salt in a measuring cup. Add all-purpose flour to measure 3/4 cup.

Five-Chip Cookies

Sharon Hedstrom, Minnetonka, Minnesota

(Pictured at left)

 With peanut butter, oats and five kinds of chips, these cookies make a hearty snack that appeals to kids of all ages. I sometimes double the recipe to share with friends and neighbors.

  1 cup butter *or* margarine, softened
  1 cup peanut butter
  1 cup sugar
2/3 cup packed brown sugar
  2 eggs
  1 teaspoon vanilla extract
  2 cups all-purpose flour
  1 cup old-fashioned oats
  2 teaspoons baking soda
1/2 teaspoon salt
2/3 cup *each* milk chocolate chips, semisweet chocolate chips, peanut butter chips, vanilla chips and butterscotch chips

In a mixing bowl, cream butter, peanut butter and sugars. Add eggs, one at a time, beating well after each addition. Beat in vanilla. Combine flour, oats, baking soda and salt; gradually add to the creamed mixture. Stir in chips. Drop by rounded tablespoonfuls 2 in. apart onto ungreased baking sheets. Bake at 350° for 10-12 minutes or until lightly browned. Cool for 1 minute before removing to wire racks. **Yield:** 4-1/2 dozen.

Orange Dreams

Susan Warren, North Manchester, Indiana

A fellow teacher shared this recipe with me. We have several great cooks on our teaching staff, and each of us takes turns bringing special treats to the lounge. These moist, chewy cookies with a pleasant orange flavor are a favorite.

  1 cup butter *or* margarine, softened
1/2 cup sugar
1/2 cup packed brown sugar
  1 egg
  1 tablespoon grated orange peel
2-1/4 cups all-purpose flour
3/4 teaspoon baking soda
1/2 teaspoon salt
1-1/2 cups vanilla chips

> **CHIP-CHIP HOORAY!** Pictured at left: Five-Chip Cookies (recipe on this page).

In a mixing bowl, cream butter and sugars. Beat in egg and orange peel. Combine flour, baking soda and salt; gradually add to the creamed mixture. Stir in vanilla chips. Drop by rounded tablespoonfuls 2 in. apart onto ungreased baking sheets. Bake at 350° for 10-12 minutes or until golden brown. Remove to wire racks to cool. **Yield:** 4-1/2 dozen.

German Spice Cookies

Joan Tyson, Bowling Green, Ohio

These chewy spice cookies are great with coffee and taste even better the next day. The recipe has been a family favorite for more than 40 years.

  3 eggs
  2 cups packed brown sugar
  1 teaspoon ground cloves
  1 teaspoon ground cinnamon
1/2 teaspoon pepper
  2 cups all-purpose flour
1/2 teaspoon baking soda
1/2 teaspoon salt
  1 cup raisins
  1 cup chopped walnuts

In a mixing bowl, beat eggs. Add the brown sugar, cloves, cinnamon and pepper. Combine flour, baking soda and salt; gradually add to the egg mixture. Stir in raisins and walnuts. Drop by tablespoonfuls 2 in. apart onto lightly greased baking sheets. Bake at 400° for 8-10 minutes or until surface cracks. Remove to wire racks to cool. **Yield:** 3-1/2 dozen. **Editor's Note:** This recipe contains no butter or shortening.

Coconut Macaroons

Naomi Vining, Springdale, Arkansas

This recipe was lost in my files for more than 40 years before I uncovered it. I decided to make these macaroons for an event at the business my husband and I own… they were a hit with everyone.

1/2 cup egg whites (about 4)
1/4 teaspoon salt
1-1/4 cups sugar
1/2 teaspoon vanilla extract
  3 cups flaked coconut

In a mixing bowl, beat egg whites and salt until soft peaks form. Gradually add sugar, beating until stiff peaks form, about 6 minutes. Beat in vanilla. Fold in coconut. Drop by rounded teaspoonfuls 2 in. apart onto lightly greased baking sheets. Bake at 325° for 20 minutes or until firm to the touch. Remove to wire racks to cool. **Yield:** 5 dozen.

Almond Drops

Lois Heemstra, Primghar, Iowa

My family—all of whom are self-proclaimed choco-holics—can't get enough of these rich cookies. My sis-ter-in-law shared the recipe and believes their success lies in beating the butter and sugar very well.

　　2 cups butter (no substitutes), softened
　　2 cups sugar
　　2 teaspoons almond extract
3-1/2 cups all-purpose flour
　　1 teaspoon baking soda
　　1/2 teaspoon baking powder
　　1/4 teaspoon salt
　　1 cup sliced almonds

In a mixing bowl, cream butter and sugar until almost white, about 10-12 minutes. Beat in extract. Combine flour, baking soda, baking powder and salt; gradual-ly add to the creamed mixture. Stir in almonds. Drop by rounded teaspoonfuls 2 in. apart onto ungreased baking sheets. Bake at 350° for 10-12 minutes or un-til lightly browned. Cool for 2 minutes before re-moving to wire racks. **Yield:** about 7 dozen.

Three-in-One Cookies

Leota Davis, Searcy, Arkansas

When my three daughters were young, they each want-ed me to make cookies with their favorite ingredient. One day I decided to combine chocolate, peanut butter and oatmeal into one cookie. They all loved the results!

　　1 cup butter-flavored shortening
　　3/4 cup sugar
　　3/4 cup packed brown sugar
　　2 eggs
　　1 teaspoon water
　　1 teaspoon vanilla extract
　　2 cups quick-cooking oats
1-1/2 cups all-purpose flour
　　1/2 cup baking cocoa
　　1 teaspoon baking soda
　　1 teaspoon salt
　　1 package (10 ounces) peanut butter chips
　　1 cup chopped nuts

In a mixing bowl, cream shortening and sugars. Add eggs, one at a time, beating well after each addition. Beat in water and vanilla. Combine oats, flour, cocoa, baking soda and salt; gradually add to the creamed mixture. Stir in peanut butter chips and nuts. Drop by tablespoonfuls 2 in. apart onto greased baking

Brown Sugar Crinkles

Donna Frame, Montgomery Village, Maryland

The addition of brown sugar makes these deliciously different from traditional sugar cookies. They're at-tractive and simple to make. The recipe can be easily cut in half.

　　1 cup butter *or* margarine, softened
　　1 cup shortening
　　3 cups sugar
1-1/2 cups packed brown sugar
　　6 eggs
　　1 tablespoon vanilla extract
　　6 cups all-purpose flour
　　1 tablespoon baking soda
1-1/2 teaspoons salt

In a mixing bowl, cream butter, shortening and sug-ars. Add eggs, one at a time, beating well after each ad-dition. Beat in vanilla. Combine flour, baking soda and salt; gradually add to the creamed mixture (the dough will be soft). Drop by rounded teaspoonfuls 2 in. apart onto ungreased baking sheets. Flatten with a glass dipped in sugar. Bake at 350° for 10-12 min-utes or until lightly browned. Cool for 2 minutes be-fore removing to wire racks. **Yield:** about 13 dozen.

Amish Raisin Cookies

Marcia Wagner, Berrien Springs, Michigan

I found this recipe for a chewy raisin cookie in one of the many Amish cookbooks I own. I haven't seen it dupli-cated anywhere else.

　　1 cup raisins
　　1 cup water
　　3/4 cup butter *or* margarine, softened
　　2 cups packed brown sugar
　　1 egg
　　1 teaspoon vanilla extract
　　3 cups all-purpose flour
　　1 teaspoon baking soda
　　1 teaspoon baking powder
　　1/8 teaspoon salt

In a small saucepan, combine raisins and water. Bring to a boil; cook until liquid is reduced to 1/2 cup. Set aside to cool. In a mixing bowl, cream butter and brown sugar. Beat in egg and vanilla. Combine flour, baking soda, baking powder and salt; gradually add to creamed mixture. Stir in raisins with liquid. Drop by tablespoonfuls 2 in. apart onto ungreased baking sheets. Bake at 375° for 10-12 minutes or until the surface cracks. Remove to wire racks to cool. **Yield:** 6 dozen.

Sweet Potato Spice Cookies

Ruth Shaffer, Elizabethville, Pennsylvania

Shredded sweet potatoes, butterscotch chips, pecans, coconut and spices are creatively combined in a one-of-a-kind cookie that always brings rave reviews.

   3/4 cup butter *or* margarine, softened
   1 cup sugar
   1/4 cup packed brown sugar
   1 egg
   1 cup finely shredded uncooked sweet potato
   3 tablespoons orange juice concentrate
   2 cups all-purpose flour
   1 teaspoon baking powder
   1 teaspoon ground cinnamon
   1/2 teaspoon baking soda
   1/2 teaspoon salt
   1/4 teaspoon ground nutmeg
1-1/4 cups quick-cooking oats
   1 cup butterscotch chips
   1 cup flaked coconut
   1 cup chopped pecans

In a mixing bowl, cream butter and sugars. Beat in egg, sweet potato and orange juice concentrate. Combine flour, baking powder, cinnamon, baking soda, salt and nutmeg; gradually add to the creamed mixture. Stir in remaining ingredients. Drop by rounded teaspoonfuls 2 in. apart onto greased baking sheets. Bake at 350° for 14-16 minutes or until firm. Remove to wire racks to cool. **Yield:** 7 dozen.

Big Chocolate Cookies

M. Marie Macy, Fort Collins, Colorado

The combination of different kinds of chocolate makes these cookies irresistible. Friends and family are delighted to have a "big" cookie to enjoy.

   6 tablespoons butter (no substitutes)
   6 squares (1 ounce *each*) semisweet chocolate
   2 squares (1 ounce *each*) unsweetened chocolate
   2 eggs
   3/4 cup sugar
   2 teaspoons instant coffee granules
   1 tablespoon boiling water
   2 teaspoons vanilla extract
1/4 cup all-purpose flour*

1/2 teaspoon salt
1/4 teaspoon baking powder
   1 cup (6 ounces) semisweet chocolate chips
   1 cup coarsely chopped walnuts
   1 cup coarsely chopped pecans

In a microwave or double boiler, melt butter and the chocolate squares; cool. In a mixing bowl, beat eggs until foamy; gradually add sugar. Dissolve coffee granules in water. Add coffee and vanilla to egg mixture. Combine flour, salt and baking powder; gradually add to the egg mixture. Stir in chocolate chips and nuts. Drop by 1/3 cupfuls 4 in. apart onto ungreased baking sheets. Bake at 350° for 15-17 minutes or until firm. Cool for 4 minutes before removing to wire racks. **Yield:** 3 dozen. ***Editor's Note:** 1/4 cup flour is the correct amount.

Chocolate Chip Sprinkle Cookies

Heidi Cretens, Milwaukee, Wisconsin

Whenever I used to make cookies, my three boys would always find something they didn't like about them. After some trial and error, I finally came up with a cookie they all enjoyed.

   2 cups butter *or* margarine, softened
   1 cup sugar
   1 cup packed brown sugar
   2 eggs
1-1/2 teaspoons vanilla extract
   4 cups all-purpose flour
   1 teaspoon baking soda
   1/2 teaspoon salt
   2 cups (12 ounces) semisweet chocolate chips
   1/2 cup quick-cooking oats
   1/2 cup crisp rice cereal
   1/2 cup colored sprinkles
   1/2 cup chopped pecans

In a mixing bowl, cream butter and sugars. Add the eggs, one at a time, beating well after each addition. Beat in vanilla. Combine the flour, baking soda and salt; gradually add to creamed mixture. Stir in remaining ingredients. Drop by rounded tablespoonfuls 2 in. apart onto greased baking sheets. Bake at 375° for 8-10 minutes or until lightly browned. Remove to wire racks to cool. **Yield:** about 7-1/2 dozen.

DROP COOKIES tend to spread quite a bit while baking, so space them out on the baking sheet as the recipe directs. To prevent cookies from spreading even more than usual, let hot baking sheets cool to room temperature before using again.

Peanut Butter Cup Cookies

Faith Jensen, Meridian, Idaho

With the classic combination of chocolate and peanut butter, it's no surprise these are my family's favorite cookies. Because of their ease of preparation, I'm able to make them at a moment's notice.

    1 cup butter *or* margarine, softened
2/3 cup peanut butter
    1 cup sugar
    1 cup packed brown sugar
    2 eggs
    2 teaspoons vanilla extract
2-1/4 cups all-purpose flour
    1 teaspoon baking soda
1/2 teaspoon salt
    2 cups (12 ounces) semisweet chocolate chips
    2 cups chopped peanut butter cups (about six 1.6-ounce packages)

In a mixing bowl, cream butter, peanut butter and sugars. Add eggs, one at a time, beating well after each addition. Beat in vanilla. Combine flour, baking soda and salt; gradually add to the creamed mixture. Stir in the chocolate chips and peanut butter cups. Drop by rounded tablespoonfuls 2 in. apart onto ungreased baking sheets. Bake at 350° for 10-12 minutes or until edges are lightly browned. Cool for 2 minutes before removing to wire racks. **Yield:** 7-1/2 dozen.

Hint o' Mint Cookies

Janet Hartmann, Gibbon, Minnesota

After I experimented in the kitchen mixing and matching ingredients to come up with a new and different cookie recipe, my husband proclaimed these the winner! With a little peppermint extract, these cake-like cookies bring a nice close to any meal.

1/2 cup milk
1/2 teaspoon vinegar
1/2 cup butter *or* margarine, softened
    1 cup sugar
    1 egg
1/2 teaspoon vanilla extract
1/4 teaspoon peppermint extract
    2 cups all-purpose flour
1/2 teaspoon baking soda
1/4 teaspoon cream of tartar
FROSTING:
    3 tablespoons butter *or* margarine, softened

    2 cups confectioners' sugar
1/3 cup baking cocoa
1/8 teaspoon salt
    1 teaspoon vanilla extract
    2 to 4 tablespoons milk

In a small bowl, combine milk and vinegar; set aside. In a mixing bowl, cream butter and sugar. Beat in egg and extracts. Combine flour, baking soda and cream of tartar; add to the creamed mixture alternately with milk mixture. Drop by heaping teaspoonfuls 2 in. apart onto ungreased baking sheets. Flatten with a glass dipped in sugar. Bake at 350° for 6-8 minutes or until set. Remove to wire racks to cool. In a small mixing bowl, cream butter, sugar, cocoa and salt. Beat in vanilla and enough milk to achieve spreading consistency. Frost cooled cookies. **Yield:** 4 dozen.

Maple Nut Date Cookies

Joyce Palmer, Klamath Falls, Oregon

I can't resist these soft cookies topped with a maple-flavored frosting. Dates, pecans and coconut add some unexpected wholesomeness.

    1 cup butter *or* margarine, softened
    3 eggs
    1 cup maple syrup
3-1/4 cups all-purpose flour
    1 teaspoon baking powder
    1 teaspoon baking soda
    1 teaspoon salt
    1 cup chopped dates
    1 cup chopped pecans
3/4 cup flaked coconut
FROSTING:
1/4 cup butter *or* margarine, softened
    1 cup confectioners' sugar
    2 tablespoons whipping cream
    1 tablespoon maple syrup
    1 teaspoon vanilla extract
1/4 teaspoon maple flavoring

In a mixing bowl, cream butter. Add eggs, one at a time, beating well after each addition. Beat in syrup (mixture will appear curdled). Combine flour, baking powder, baking soda and salt; gradually add to the creamed mixture. Stir in dates, pecans and coconut. Cover and refrigerate for 2 hours or until easy to handle. Drop by rounded teaspoonfuls 2 in. apart onto greased baking sheets. Bake at 350° for 9-11 minutes or until edges are lightly browned. Cool for 2 minutes before removing to wire racks. In a small mixing bowl, cream butter and sugar. Beat in cream, syrup, vanilla and maple flavoring until smooth. Frost cooled cookies. **Yield:** about 8 dozen.

Lemon Drop Cookies

Pat Zimmerman, Midland, Texas

After we'd visited at her house, my sister sent a "care" package for the trip home. Tucked inside were these delightful cookies. Crushed lemon drop candies and grated lemon peel lend to the refreshing taste.

  1/2 cup butter (no substitutes), softened
  3/4 cup sugar
   1 egg
   1 tablespoon half-and-half cream
   1 teaspoon grated lemon peel
1-1/2 cups all-purpose flour
  1/2 cup finely crushed lemon drops
   1 teaspoon baking powder
  1/4 teaspoon salt

In a mixing bowl, cream butter and sugar. Beat in egg, cream and lemon peel. Combine flour, lemon drops, baking powder and salt; gradually add to the creamed mixture. Drop by rounded teaspoonfuls 3 in. apart onto greased baking sheets. Bake at 350° for 8-10 minutes or until edges are lightly browned. Cool for 2 minutes before removing to wire racks. **Yield:** about 3-1/2 dozen.

Nutty Butter Munchies

Zenola Frazier, Tallulah, Louisiana

I developed this recipe for a crisp cookie as a way to satisfy my sweet tooth. Peanuts and pecans are abundant here in Louisiana, so I bake with them often.

   1 cup butter *or* margarine, softened
  1/2 cup chunky peanut butter
   1 cup sugar
   1 cup packed brown sugar
   3 eggs
   1 teaspoon vanilla extract
  1/2 teaspoon lemon extract
  1/2 teaspoon almond extract
   3 cups all-purpose flour
  1/2 teaspoon baking soda
  1/2 teaspoon salt
1-1/2 cups chopped pecans
  1/2 cup salted peanuts

In a mixing bowl, cream butter, peanut butter and sugars. Add eggs, one at a time, beating well after each addition. Beat in extracts. Combine flour, baking soda and salt; gradually add to the creamed mixture. Stir in nuts. Drop by tablespoonfuls 2 in. apart onto greased baking sheets. Flatten with a glass dipped in

sugar. Bake at 350° for 10-12 minutes or until the edges are lightly browned. Remove to wire racks to cool. **Yield:** 8-1/2 dozen.

Chewy Raisin Molasses Cookies

Ranell Sturm, Clements, California

Molasses adds a little more flavor to a traditional oatmeal raisin cookie. My husband loves the soft and chewy texture of these cookies. The recipe is from his mother.

1-1/2 cups raisins
  1/2 cup shortening
1-1/4 cups sugar
   2 eggs
  1/2 cup molasses
   2 cups quick-cooking oats
1-3/4 cups all-purpose flour
   1 teaspoon baking soda
   1 teaspoon salt
   1 teaspoon ground cinnamon

Place raisins in a bowl. Cover with boiling water; let stand for 5 minutes. Drain and set aside. In a mixing bowl, cream shortening and sugar. Add eggs, one at a time, beating well after each addition. Beat in molasses. Combine oats, flour, baking soda, salt and cinnamon; gradually add to the creamed mixture. Stir in raisins. Drop by tablespoonfuls 2 in. apart onto lightly greased baking sheets. Bake at 350° for 12-14 minutes or until lightly browned. Remove to wire racks to cool. **Yield:** about 5 dozen.

Potato Chip Crunchies

Dorothy Buiter, Worth, Illinois

I usually have all sorts of baked goodies waiting for my family when they come home for the holidays. No matter how fancy the other cookies are, these are usually the first to go.

   2 cups butter *or* margarine, softened
1-1/2 cups sugar
   1 egg
   1 teaspoon vanilla extract
   4 cups all-purpose flour
   1 cup crushed potato chips
   1 cup chopped pecans

In a mixing bowl, cream butter and sugar. Beat in egg and vanilla. Gradually add flour. Fold in the potato chips and pecans. Drop by tablespoonfuls 1-1/2 in. apart onto ungreased baking sheets. Flatten with a fork. Bake at 350° for 12-14 minutes or until golden brown. Remove to wire racks to cool. **Yield:** 8 dozen.

German Chocolate Toffee Cookies

Joyce Robb, Dillon, Montana

(Pictured at left)

When I first shared these crisp cookies with folks at the hospital where I work as a cook, everyone's palate was pleased! German sweet chocolate gives them a unique twist.

    1 cup butter (no substitutes), softened
    1 cup shortening
2-1/2 cups sugar
  1/2 cup packed brown sugar
    1 package (4 ounces) German sweet chocolate,
      melted
    4 eggs
    2 teaspoons water
    2 teaspoons vanilla extract
6-1/2 cups all-purpose flour
    2 teaspoons baking soda
1-1/2 teaspoons salt
1-1/2 cups English toffee bits *or* almond brickle
      chips
1-1/2 cups chopped walnuts

In a mixing bowl, cream butter, shortening and sugars. Beat in chocolate. Add eggs, one at a time, beating well after each addition. Beat in water and vanilla. Combine flour, baking soda and salt; gradually add to the creamed mixture. Stir in toffee bits and walnuts. Drop by tablespoonfuls 2 in. apart onto greased baking sheets. Bake at 350° for 12-15 minutes or until golden brown. Remove to wire racks to cool. **Yield:** 13 dozen.

Cherry Almond Chews

Alma Chaney, Trenton, Ohio

(Pictured at left)

I make these attractive cherry coconut cookies every Christmas for family and friends. During that busy time of year, I appreciate the fact that they freeze well, so I can make them ahead.

    1 cup shortening
    1 cup sugar
    1 cup packed brown sugar
    2 eggs
  3/4 teaspoon almond extract

COOKIES-AND-MILK MEMORIES. Pictured at left, top to bottom: German Chocolate Toffee Cookies and Cherry Almond Chews (both recipes on this page).

2-1/2 cups all-purpose flour
    1 teaspoon baking soda
    1 teaspoon salt
2-1/2 cups flaked coconut
  3/4 cup chopped almonds *or* pecans, optional
    1 jar (16 ounces) maraschino cherries, drained
      and halved

In a mixing bowl, cream shortening and sugars. Add eggs, one at a time, beating well after each addition. Beat in extract. Combine flour, baking soda and salt; gradually add to the creamed mixture. Stir in coconut and nuts if desired. Drop by rounded teaspoonfuls 2 in. apart onto lightly greased baking sheets. Place a cherry half in the center of each. Bake at 350° for 12-14 minutes or until lightly browned. Remove to wire racks to cool. **Yield:** about 7 dozen.

Frosted Raisin Nut Cookies

Peg Wiechman, Hubbard, Iowa

This old-fashioned cookie is topped with an irresistible brown sugar frosting. I've had the recipe for more than 45 years and have given it out countless times.

    1 cup raisins
1-1/2 cups boiling water
    1 cup shortening
    1 cup sugar
    2 eggs
    1 teaspoon vanilla extract
    3 cups all-purpose flour
    1 teaspoon baking soda
  1/8 teaspoon salt
  1/2 cup chopped walnuts
BROWN SUGAR FROSTING:
    6 to 8 tablespoons whipping cream, *divided*
  1/4 cup packed brown sugar
    2 tablespoons butter *or* margarine
    2 cups confectioners' sugar

Place raisins in a bowl. Add boiling water; let stand for 5 minutes. Drain, reserving 1/4 cup liquid; set the raisins and liquid aside. In a mixing bowl, cream shortening and sugar. Add eggs, one at a time, beating well after each addition. Beat in vanilla. Combine flour, baking soda and salt; add to the creamed mixture alternately with reserved liquid. Stir in walnuts and raisins. Drop by rounded teaspoonfuls 2 in. apart onto ungreased baking sheets. Bake at 375° for 9-11 minutes or until lightly browned. Cool for 2 minutes before removing to wire racks to cool. In a small saucepan, combine 4 tablespoons cream, brown sugar and butter. Cook and stir until mixture comes to a full boil; boil for 1 minute. Place confectioners' sugar in a mixing bowl; add hot cream mixture and enough of the remaining cream to achieve spreading consistency. Frost cooled cookies. **Yield:** 6-1/2 dozen.

Cookie Jar Nut Cookies

Mrs. Terry Robbins, Hendersonville, North Carolina

I started collecting cookie recipes when I was a teenager. These chewy spice cookies were some of the first I ever made, and they're still a favorite today. They can be found in my cookie jar whenever someone stops by.

    1 cup butter *or* margarine, softened
    2 cups packed brown sugar
    2 eggs
 1/4 cup milk
    1 teaspoon vanilla extract
    3 cups all-purpose flour
    1 teaspoon baking soda
    1 teaspoon salt
    1 teaspoon ground nutmeg
    1 cup chopped walnuts

In a mixing bowl, cream butter and brown sugar. Add eggs, one at a time, beating well after each addition. Beat in milk and vanilla. Combine flour, baking soda, salt and nutmeg; gradually add to the creamed mixture. Stir in walnuts. Drop by rounded teaspoonfuls 2 in. apart onto ungreased baking sheets. Flatten with a glass dipped in sugar. Bake at 350° for 10-12 minutes or until lightly browned. Remove to wire racks to cool. **Yield:** 9 dozen.

Iced Orange Cookies

Lori DiPietro, New Port Richey, Florida

I usually make these bite-size cookies at Christmastime, when oranges in Florida are plentiful. Every time I sniff their wonderful aroma, I remember my grandmother, who shared the recipe.

 1/2 cup shortening
    1 cup sugar
    2 eggs
 1/2 cup orange juice
    1 tablespoon grated orange peel
2-1/2 cups all-purpose flour
1-1/2 teaspoons baking powder
 1/2 teaspoon salt
ICING:
    2 cups confectioners' sugar
 1/4 cup orange juice
    2 tablespoons butter (no substitutes), melted

In a mixing bowl, cream shortening and sugar. Add eggs, one at a time, beating well after each addition. Beat in orange juice and peel. Combine flour, baking powder and salt; gradually add to the creamed mixture. Drop by heaping teaspoonfuls 2 in. apart onto ungreased baking sheets. Bake at 350° for 10-12 minutes or until edges begin to brown. Remove to wire racks to cool. In a small bowl, combine icing ingredients until smooth; drizzle over cooled cookies. **Yield:** about 5-1/2 dozen.

Kitchen Sink Cookies

Jean Lucas, Elkhart, Indiana

These cookies are loaded with lots of tasty ingredients—everything but the kitchen sink! Everyone in our family knows you have to be quick on the draw to get your share. Even though the recipe makes a big batch, folks are left asking, "Where did all the cookies go?"

    1 cup butter (no substitutes), softened
    1 cup vegetable oil
    1 cup sugar
    1 cup packed brown sugar
    2 eggs
    1 tablespoon vanilla extract
3-1/2 cups all-purpose flour
    1 teaspoon salt
    1 teaspoon cream of tartar
    1 teaspoon baking soda
    1 cup quick-cooking oats
    1 cup crisp rice cereal
    1 cup flaked coconut
    1 cup butterscotch chips
    1 cup raisins
    1 cup chopped walnuts

In a mixing bowl, cream butter, oil and sugars. Add eggs, one at a time, beating well after each addition. Beat in vanilla. Combine flour, salt, cream of tartar and baking soda; gradually add to the creamed mixture. Stir in the remaining ingredients. Drop by level tablespoonfuls 2 in. apart onto ungreased baking sheets. Bake at 350° for 11-13 minutes or until lightly browned. Remove to wire racks to cool. **Yield:** 9 dozen.

Sponge Cake Cookies

Terry Carpenter, Vineland, New Jersey

My heart's warmed by these cookies because the recipe comes from my grandmother. No wedding, shower or holiday gathering went by without our caring matriarch or her pretty little treats.

    1 cup butter *or* margarine, softened
1-1/2 cups sugar
    8 eggs

        2 tablespoons lemon extract
        4 cups all-purpose flour
        1/4 cup baking powder
FROSTING:
        1/2 cup butter *or* margarine, softened
3-3/4 cups confectioners' sugar
        1 teaspoon lemon extract
        1/8 teaspoon salt
        3 to 4 tablespoons milk
Food coloring, optional
        4 cups flaked coconut, optional

In a mixing bowl, cream butter and sugar. Add eggs, one at a time, beating well after each addition. Beat in extract. Combine flour and baking powder; gradually add to the creamed mixture. Drop by teaspoonfuls 3 in. apart onto ungreased baking sheets. Bake at 400° for 6-8 minutes or until the edges are lightly browned. Remove to wire racks to cool. In a mixing bowl, cream butter, sugar, extract and salt. Add enough milk to achieve spreading consistency. Tint with food coloring if desired. Frost cooled cookies. Sprinkle with coconut if desired. **Yield:** 11 dozen.

Hearty Whole Wheat Cookies

Lynore Derkson, Airdrie, Alberta

My grandchildren would do just about anything for one of these cookies. Packed with chocolate chips and peanuts, they're made with oats and whole wheat flour, so I don't mind them nibbling on them.

        1 cup butter (no substitutes), softened
        2 cups packed brown sugar
        3 eggs
        3 tablespoons half-and-half cream
        2 teaspoons vanilla extract
        2 cups quick-cooking oats
        2 cups whole wheat flour
        1 teaspoon baking soda
        1 teaspoon baking powder
        1/2 teaspoon salt
        1 package (12 ounces) miniature semisweet
            chocolate chips
        2 cups coarsely chopped peanuts

In a mixing bowl, cream butter and brown sugar. Add eggs, one at a time, beating well after each addition. Beat in the cream and vanilla. In a blender or food processor, process oats until finely ground. Combine oats, flour, baking soda, baking powder and salt; gradually add to the creamed mixture. Stir in chocolate chips and peanuts. Drop by tablespoonfuls 1-1/2 in. apart onto ungreased baking sheets. Bake at 350° for 10-12 minutes or until golden brown. Remove to wire racks to cool. **Yield:** 6 dozen.

Blueberry Oat Cookies

Elaine Gelina, Ladson, South Carolina

It's fun to make these cookies at the height of blueberry season when folks are looking for tasty ways to serve that juicy fruit. A hint of cinnamon adds a special touch.

        1/2 cup butter *or* margarine, softened
        1 cup packed brown sugar
        1 egg
        1 teaspoon vanilla extract
1-1/2 cups quick-cooking oats
        1 cup all-purpose flour
        1 to 2 teaspoons ground cinnamon
        1/2 teaspoon salt
        1/2 teaspoon baking soda
        1/4 teaspoon baking powder
        1 cup fresh *or* frozen blueberries

In a mixing bowl, cream butter and brown sugar. Beat in egg and vanilla. Combine oats, flour, cinnamon, salt, baking soda and baking powder; gradually add to the creamed mixture. Stir in the blueberries. Drop by heaping tablespoonfuls 2 in. apart onto lightly greased baking sheets. Bake at 350° for 12-14 minutes or until golden brown. Remove to wire racks to cool. **Yield:** 3 dozen.

Apricot Almond Blondies

Amy Forkner, Cheyenne, Wyoming

My mom shared this recipe with me after sampling these cookies at a bed-and-breakfast. For a little variation, I sometimes substitute cranberries and pecans for the apricots and almonds.

        3/4 cup butter *or* margarine, softened
        1 cup packed brown sugar
        1 egg
        1 teaspoon vanilla extract
1-2/3 cups all-purpose flour
        1/2 teaspoon baking soda
        1/4 teaspoon salt
        1 package (12 ounces) vanilla chips
        3/4 cup chopped almonds
        3/4 cup chopped dried apricots

In a mixing bowl, cream butter and brown sugar. Beat in egg and vanilla. Combine flour, baking soda and salt; gradually add to the creamed mixture. Stir in vanilla chips, almonds and apricots. Drop by heaping tablespoonfuls 2 in. apart onto ungreased baking sheets. Bake at 350° for 7-9 minutes or until lightly browned. Remove to wire racks to cool. **Yield:** 6 dozen.

Coffee Almond Crisps

Sarah Benthien, Wauwatosa, Wisconsin

The blend of coffee, cinnamon and toasted almonds has made these cookies a favorite for over 50 years. These crispy treats make good coffee "dunking" cookies.

- 1 cup shortening
- 2 cups packed brown sugar
- 2 eggs
- 1/2 cup brewed coffee, room temperature
- 3-1/2 cups all-purpose flour
- 1 teaspoon baking soda
- 1 teaspoon salt
- 1-1/2 teaspoons ground cinnamon, *divided*
- 1 cup chopped almonds, toasted
- 3 tablespoons sugar

In a mixing bowl, cream shortening and brown sugar. Add eggs, one at a time, beating well after each addition. Beat in coffee. Combine flour, baking soda, salt and 1 teaspoon of cinnamon; gradually add to the creamed mixture. Stir in almonds. Drop by rounded teaspoonfuls 2 in. apart onto ungreased baking sheets. Combine sugar and remaining cinnamon; sprinkle over cookies. Flatten slightly. Bake at 375° for 10-12 minutes or until firm. Remove to wire racks to cool. **Yield:** 6 dozen.

Frosted Peanut Cookies

Alicia Surma, Tacoma, Washington

Oats, chopped peanuts and peanut butter frosting make this a nice change of pace from a traditional peanut butter cookie. After folks sample these, compliments and recipe requests always follow.

- 1 cup butter *or* margarine, softened
- 1-1/2 cups packed brown sugar
- 2 eggs
- 1 teaspoon vanilla extract
- 2 cups all-purpose flour
- 2 teaspoons baking powder
- 1 cup quick-cooking oats
- 1 cup coarsely chopped salted peanuts

FROSTING:
- 1/2 cup peanut butter
- 3 cups confectioners' sugar
- 1/3 cup milk

In a mixing bowl, cream butter and brown sugar. Add eggs, one at a time, beating well after each addition. Beat in vanilla. Combine flour and baking powder; gradually add to the creamed mixture. Stir in oats and

peanuts. Drop by rounded teaspoonfuls 2 in. apart onto ungreased baking sheets. Bake at 350° for 10-12 minutes or until golden brown. Remove to wire racks to cool. In a mixing bowl, combine frosting ingredients; beat until smooth. Frost cooled cookies. **Yield:** 5 dozen.

Chocolate Raspberry Cookies

Sherri Crotwell, Shasta Lake, California

I moved away from a dear friend some years ago. Knowing she loved raspberries, I created this recipe. Now I send her these cookies to help her remember the fun times we had together.

- 1 cup butter *or* margarine, softened
- 3/4 cup sugar
- 3/4 cup packed brown sugar
- 2 eggs
- 3/4 cup semisweet chocolate chips, melted and cooled
- 1/2 cup raspberries, pureed
- 3 cups all-purpose flour
- 3/4 teaspoon baking soda
- 3/4 teaspoon salt
- 1 cup vanilla chips

In a mixing bowl, cream butter and sugars. Add eggs, one at a time, beating well after each addition. Beat in melted chocolate and raspberries. Combine the flour, baking soda and salt; gradually add to the creamed mixture. Stir in vanilla chips. Drop by teaspoonfuls 2 in. apart onto ungreased baking sheets. Bake at 375° for 10-12 minutes or until edges begin to brown. Remove to wire racks to cool. **Yield:** 6 dozen.

Pineapple Delights

Jack Stubblefield, East Canton, Ohio

When I was stationed in Germany, my mother would often send these tropical-tasting cookies to me. The recipe is special because it came from my grandmother. Now my wife and daughter are carrying on the tradition.

- 1 cup butter *or* margarine, softened
- 1 cup sugar
- 1 cup packed brown sugar
- 2 eggs
- 1 teaspoon vanilla extract
- 4 cups all-purpose flour
- 2 teaspoons baking powder
- 1/2 teaspoon baking soda
- 1/2 teaspoon salt
- 1 can (8 ounces) crushed pineapple, drained

1 cup chopped walnuts
1/4 cup chopped maraschino cherries

In a mixing bowl, cream butter and sugars. Add the eggs, one at a time, beating well after each addition. Beat in vanilla. Combine flour, baking powder, baking soda and salt; gradually add to the creamed mixture. Stir in pineapple, walnuts and cherries. Drop by rounded tablespoonfuls 2 in. apart onto ungreased baking sheets. Bake at 425° for 7-9 minutes or until lightly browned. Remove to wire racks to cool. **Yield:** 7 dozen.

Apple Doodles

Cecilia Lorraine Ruiz, Sunnyvale, California

This originally started as an apple cake recipe. But I worked it into a recipe for cookies and have been making them this way ever since. It's a nice way to feature fall's delicious produce.

2/3 cup butter-flavored shortening
1 cup sugar
1 egg
1 teaspoon vanilla extract
2 cups all-purpose flour
2-1/4 teaspoons ground cinnamon
1 teaspoon baking powder
1 teaspoon baking soda
1/2 teaspoon salt
1 cup finely diced peeled tart apple
3/4 cup chopped walnuts, optional

In a mixing bowl, cream shortening and sugar. Beat in egg and vanilla. Combine the flour, cinnamon, baking powder, baking soda and salt; stir half into the creamed mixture. Stir in apple, walnuts if desired and the remaining dry ingredients. Drop by heaping teaspoonfuls 3 in. apart onto lightly greased baking sheets. Bake at 375° for 13-15 minutes or until golden brown. Remove to wire racks to cool. **Yield:** 3-1/2 dozen.

Chocolate Marshmallow Meltaways

Joanna Swartley, Harrisonburg, Virginia

Kids are thrilled to find a marshmallow hidden under this cookie's cocoa frosting. I enjoyed these cookies as a child, and now my own family loves them, too.

1/2 cup butter-flavored shortening
3/4 cup sugar
1 egg
1/4 cup milk
1 teaspoon vanilla extract
1-3/4 cups all-purpose flour

1/2 cup baking cocoa
1/2 teaspoon baking soda
1/2 teaspoon salt
18 large marshmallows, halved
FROSTING:
3 tablespoons butter *or* margarine, softened
3 cups confectioners' sugar
3 tablespoons baking cocoa
1/8 teaspoon salt
4 to 6 tablespoons milk

In a mixing bowl, cream shortening and sugar. Beat in egg, milk and vanilla. Combine flour, cocoa, baking soda and salt; gradually add to the creamed mixture. Drop by tablespoonfuls 2 in. apart onto ungreased baking sheets. Bake at 350° for 8 minutes. Press a marshmallow, cut side down, onto each cookie. Bake 2 minutes longer. Remove to wire racks to cool. In a mixing bowl, cream butter, sugar, cocoa and salt. Add enough milk to achieve spreading consistency. Frost cooled cookies. **Yield:** 3 dozen.

Ambrosia Bites

Arlene Steinwart, Grand Island, Nebraska

These chewy oatmeal cookies are packed with the refreshing flavors of orange and lemon, plus dates, raisins and coconut. When our children, grandchildren and great-grandchildren ask me to make "Grandma's Cookies", these are the ones they're referring to.

1 cup butter *or* margarine, softened
1 cup sugar
1 cup packed brown sugar
2 eggs
1 tablespoon grated orange peel
1 tablespoon grated lemon peel
1 teaspoon vanilla extract
2 cups all-purpose flour
1-1/2 cups quick-cooking oats
1-1/2 teaspoons baking soda
1 teaspoon baking powder
1 teaspoon salt
1 cup chopped walnuts
1 cup raisins
1 cup chopped dates
1 cup flaked coconut

In a mixing bowl, cream butter and sugars. Add the eggs, one at a time, beating well after each addition. Beat in peels and vanilla. Combine flour, oats, baking soda, baking powder and salt; gradually add to the creamed mixture. Stir in remaining ingredients. Drop by heaping tablespoonfuls 3 in. apart onto ungreased baking sheets. Bake at 375° for 8-10 minutes or until golden brown. Remove to wire racks to cool. **Yield:** 6 dozen.

Cutout Classics

Shortbread Cutouts

Jean Henderson, Montgomery, Texas
(Pictured at left)

I found this recipe in a magazine over 30 years ago and have made the cutouts for Christmas ever since. Four ingredients make them an oh-so-simple recipe to whip up during the hectic holidays.

> 1 cup butter (no substitutes), softened
> 1/2 cup sugar
> 2-1/2 cups all-purpose flour
> Colored sugar, optional

In a mixing bowl, cream butter and sugar; gradually add flour. Divide dough in half. On a lightly floured surface, roll out each portion to 1/4-in. thickness. Cut with 2-in. to 3-in. cookie cutters dipped in flour. Place 1 in. apart on ungreased baking sheets. Sprinkle with colored sugar if desired. Bake at 300° for 20-25 minutes or until lightly browned. Remove to wire racks to cool. **Yield:** about 2 dozen.

Fruit 'n' Spice Rounds

Allison Bell, Helena, Montana
(Pictured at left)

 While looking for a way to use an abundance of dates I had on hand, I came across this recipe. With raisins and walnuts—and a delectable lemon glaze—these quickly became a family favorite.

> 1 cup butter (no substitutes), softened
> 1-1/2 cups sugar
> 3 eggs
> 3 cups all-purpose flour
> 2 teaspoons ground cinnamon
> 1 teaspoon baking soda
> 1 teaspoon ground cloves
> 1 teaspoon ground nutmeg
> 1-1/2 cups finely chopped dates
> 1 cup finely chopped raisins

COOKIE CUTTER CREATIONS. Pictured at left, top to bottom: Fruit 'n' Spice Rounds and Shortbread Cutouts (both recipes on this page).

> 1 cup finely chopped walnuts
> GLAZE:
> 2 cups confectioners' sugar
> 2 tablespoons lemon juice
> 2 tablespoons water

In a mixing bowl, cream butter and sugar. Add eggs, one at a time, beating well after each addition. Combine flour, cinnamon, baking soda, cloves and nutmeg; gradually add to the creamed mixture. Stir in the dates, raisins and walnuts. Cover and refrigerate for 2 hours or until easy to handle. On a floured surface, roll out to 1/4-in. thickness. Cut with a 2-1/2-in. round cookie cutter dipped in flour. Place 1 in. apart on greased baking sheets. Bake at 375° for 10-12 minutes. Remove to wire racks. Meanwhile, combine glaze ingredients; brush over warm cookies. **Yield:** 5 dozen.

Soft Molasses Cutout Cookies

Vivian Person, Balaton, Minnesota

I received this recipe years ago, when my husband and I managed a retirement home. We'd always put out homemade cookies for morning and afternoon coffee, and these were the first to disappear.

> 1 cup shortening
> 1/2 cup sugar
> 1/2 cup packed brown sugar
> 2 eggs
> 1 cup dark molasses
> 5-1/2 cups all-purpose flour
> 1 tablespoon baking soda
> 1 teaspoon ground ginger
> 1 teaspoon ground cinnamon
> 3/4 teaspoon salt
> 1/2 cup water
> Frosting *or* confectioners' sugar, optional

In a mixing bowl, cream shortening and sugars. Add eggs, one at a time, beating well after each addition. Beat in molasses. Combine flour, baking soda, ginger, cinnamon and salt; add to the creamed mixture alternately with water. Cover and refrigerate for 3 hours or until easy to handle. On a lightly floured surface, roll out to 1/4-in. thickness. Cut with 2-1/2-in. cookie cutters dipped in flour. Place 1 in. apart on greased baking sheets. Bake at 350° for 8-10 minutes or until edges are firm. Remove to wire racks to cool. Frost or dust with confectioners' sugar if desired. **Yield:** about 6-1/2 dozen.

Surprise Cookies

Charmaine Martin, Corpus Christi, Texas

Cottage cheese is the secret ingredient in these tender, flaky cookies. I'm not sure where the recipe came from. But my grandfather was a baker, so I like to believe it was one of his.

>   1 cup butter (no substitutes), softened
> 3/4 cup small-curd cottage cheese
>   2 cups all-purpose flour
>   1 egg, beaten
>   1 cup finely chopped walnuts
> 1/2 cup sugar
> 1/8 teaspoon ground cinnamon

In a mixing bowl, cream butter and cottage cheese until smooth; gradually add flour. Cover and refrigerate for 2 hours or until easy to handle. On a lightly floured surface, roll out to 1/8-in. thickness. Cut with a 2-in. round cookie cutter dipped in flour. Place 1 in. apart on ungreased baking sheets. Brush tops with egg. Combine walnuts, sugar and cinnamon; sprinkle over cookies. Bake at 350° for 15-20 minutes or until golden brown. Remove to wire racks to cool. **Yield:** 6 dozen.

Glazed Anise Cookies

Armetta Keeney, Carlisle, Iowa

Years ago, my German neighbor made similar cookies and hung them on her Christmas tree for the neighbor kids to eat. I finally came up with my own recipe and have been very pleased with the results.

> 2/3 cup butter (no substitutes), softened
>   1 cup sugar
>   2 eggs
>   1 tablespoon aniseed
>   2 teaspoons anise extract
> 2-1/2 cups all-purpose flour
>   1 teaspoon baking powder
> 1/2 teaspoon salt
> GLAZE:
>   2 cups sugar
>   1 cup hot water
> 1/8 teaspoon cream of tartar
>   1 teaspoon anise extract
> 2-1/2 to 3 cups confectioners' sugar

In a mixing bowl, cream butter and sugar. Add eggs, one at a time, beating well after each addition. Beat in aniseed and extract. Combine flour, baking powder and salt; gradually add to the creamed mixture. Cover and refrigerate for 1 hour or until easy to han-

dle. On a lightly floured surface, roll out to 1/4-in. thickness. Cut with 2-1/2-in. cookie cutters dipped in flour. Place 1 in. apart on ungreased baking sheets. Bake 375° for 10-12 minutes or until lightly browned. Remove to wire racks to cool. In a saucepan, combine sugar, water and cream of tartar; bring to a boil over low heat. Cook and stir until a candy thermometer reads 226° (thread stage). Cool to 110° (do not stir). Stir in extract and enough confectioners' sugar to achieve spreading consistency. Spread over cookies. **Yield:** about 6 dozen.

Cinnamon Stars

Jean Jones, Peachtree City, Georgia

These cookies fill your home with an irresistible aroma as they bake. My grandmother made them every Christmas when I was a child. I have fond memories of helping her in the kitchen.

>   1 cup butter (no substitutes), softened
>   2 cups sugar
>   2 eggs
> 2-3/4 cups all-purpose flour
> 1/3 cup ground cinnamon

In a mixing bowl, cream butter and sugar. Add eggs, one at a time, beating well after each addition. Combine flour and cinnamon; gradually add to creamed mixture. Cover and refrigerate for 1 hour or until easy to handle. On a lightly floured surface, roll out to 1/4-in. thickness. Cut with a 2-1/2-in. star-shaped cookie cutter dipped in flour. Place 1 in. apart on ungreased baking sheets. Bake at 350° for 15-18 minutes or until edges are firm and bottom of cookies are lightly browned. Remove to wire racks to cool. **Yield:** 5 dozen.

Tea Cakes with Butter Frosting

Sandy Glenn, Booneville, Mississippi

This is an old-fashioned recipe that was given to me by a friend's grandmother. You can easily tint the frosting with food coloring for a festive look throughout the year.

>   1 cup butter (no substitutes), softened
>   2 cups sugar
>   3 eggs
>   1 teaspoon vanilla extract
>   5 cups all-purpose flour
>   2 teaspoons baking powder
>   1 teaspoon baking soda
> 1/4 teaspoon salt
>   1 cup buttermilk
> FROSTING:
> 1/2 cup butter (no substitutes), softened

4 cups confectioners' sugar
1 teaspoon vanilla extract
3 to 5 tablespoons milk
Food coloring, optional

In a mixing bowl, cream butter and sugar. Add eggs, one at a time, beating well after each addition. Beat in vanilla. Combine flour, baking powder, baking soda and salt; add to the creamed mixture alternately with buttermilk. Cover and refrigerate for 1 hour or until easy to handle. On a lightly floured surface, roll out to 1/4-in. thickness. Cut with 2-1/2-in. cookie cutters dipped in flour. Using a floured spatula, place 1 in. apart on greased baking sheets. Bake at 350° for 8-10 minutes or until lightly browned. Remove to wire racks to cool. In a mixing bowl, cream butter, sugar, vanilla and enough milk to achieve spreading consistency. Add food coloring if desired. Frost the cookies. **Yield:** about 5-1/2 dozen.

Almond Oatmeal Cutouts

Martha Dahlman, Regina, Saskatchewan

Almond gives these cutout oatmeal cookies added flavor. The dough is slightly sticky, so roll out the dough between pieces of waxed paper.

1/2 cup butter *or* margarine, softened
1/2 cup shortening
3/4 cup sugar
2 teaspoons almond extract
1-3/4 cups all-purpose flour
1-1/4 cups old-fashioned oats

In a mixing bowl, cream butter, shortening and sugar. Beat in extract. Combine flour and oats; gradually add to the creamed mixture. Roll out between waxed paper to 1/4-in. thickness. Cut with 2-1/2-in. cookie cutters dipped in flour. Place 1 in. apart on ungreased baking sheets. Bake at 350° for 12-15 minutes or until lightly browned. Remove to wire racks to cool. **Yield:** 2-1/2 dozen.

Butterscotch Gingerbread Men

Jane McLean, Birmingham, Alabama

The addition of butterscotch pudding makes these a little different than most gingerbread cutout recipes. The recipe comes from my mother-in-law's files.

1/2 cup butter (no substitutes), softened
1/2 cup packed brown sugar
1 package (3.4 ounces) instant butterscotch pudding mix
1 egg
1-1/2 cups all-purpose flour

1-1/2 teaspoons ground ginger
1/2 teaspoon baking soda
1/2 teaspoon ground cinnamon
FROSTING:
2 cups confectioners' sugar
3 tablespoons milk
Assorted decorator candies
Raisins

In a mixing bowl, cream butter, brown sugar and pudding mix. Beat in egg. Combine flour, ginger, baking soda and cinnamon; gradually add to the creamed mixture. Cover and refrigerate overnight. On a lightly floured surface, roll out to 1/8-in. thickness. Cut with a 5-in. gingerbread man cutter. Place 1 in. apart on ungreased baking sheets. Bake at 350° for 8-10 minutes or until edges are golden. Remove to wire racks to cool. In a mixing bowl, combine confectioners' sugar and milk until smooth. Frost and decorate cookies as desired. **Yield:** 1-1/2 dozen.

Frosted Molasses Cookies

Sarah Byler, Harrisville, Pennsylvania

If my family knows I've baked these cookies, they're sure to gobble them up in a hurry.

1 cup butter (no substitutes), softened
1 cup sugar
3 egg yolks
1 cup molasses
1/2 cup water
5 cups all-purpose flour
3 teaspoons baking soda
1-1/2 teaspoons ground cinnamon
1 teaspoon baking powder
FROSTING:
1-1/2 cups sugar
1/4 cup water
3 egg whites
1 cup confectioners' sugar

In a mixing bowl, cream butter and sugar. Beat in egg yolks, molasses and water. Combine flour, baking soda, cinnamon and baking powder; gradually add to the creamed mixture. Cover and refrigerate for 2 hours or until easy to handle. On a lightly floured surface, roll out to 1/8-in. thickness. Cut with 2-1/2-in. cookie cutters dipped in flour. Place 1 in. apart on ungreased baking sheets. Bake at 375° for 8-10 minutes or until edges are firm. Remove to wire racks to cool. In a saucepan, combine sugar and water. Cook and stir over medium heat until a candy thermometer reads 240° (soft-ball stage). In a mixing bowl, beat egg whites until stiff peaks form. Gradually add sugar syrup, beating until stiff. Beat in confectioners' sugar. Frost the cookies. Let dry on wire racks. **Yield:** 8 dozen.

Lemon Cutouts

Bonnie Lytle, Coal Township, Pennsylvania

My grandmother passed away when I was 5 years old, so I treasure this recipe of hers. Grated lemon peel adds a refreshing flavor that makes these cookies stand out from other butter cookies.

>   1 cup butter (no substitutes), softened
> 1-1/4 cups sugar
>   2 eggs
>   2 teaspoons vanilla extract
> 3-1/2 cups all-purpose flour
>   2 teaspoons baking powder
>   1/2 teaspoon grated lemon peel
> Yellow colored sugar, optional

In a mixing bowl, cream butter and sugar. Add eggs, one at a time, beating well after each addition. Beat in vanilla. Combine flour, baking powder and lemon peel; gradually add to the creamed mixture. Cover and refrigerate for 1 hour or until easy to handle. On a lightly floured surface, roll out to 1/8-in. thickness. Cut with 2-1/2-in. cookie cutters dipped in flour. Place 1 in. apart on ungreased baking sheets. Sprinkle with colored sugar if desired. Bake at 350° for 8-10 minutes or until golden brown. Remove to wire racks to cool. **Yield:** about 6 dozen.

Frosted Ginger Cookies

Barbara Larson, Minneapolis, Minnesota

A glossy white frosting gives these cookies just the right amount of sweetness. My grandmother shared the recipe with me as part of a wedding shower gift almost 40 years ago.

>   1 cup shortening
>   1 cup molasses
>   3 cups all-purpose flour
>   2 teaspoons baking soda
>   1 teaspoon salt
>   1/2 teaspoon ground ginger
>   1/4 teaspoon ground nutmeg
>   1/4 teaspoon ground cloves
> FROSTING:
>   3/4 cup water
>   1 envelope unflavored gelatin
>   3/4 cup sugar
>   3/4 cup confectioners' sugar
>   1 teaspoon baking powder
>   1 teaspoon vanilla extract

In a mixing bowl, combine shortening and molasses. Combine flour, baking soda, salt, ginger, nutmeg and

cloves; gradually add to the creamed mixture. Cover and refrigerate for 2 hours or until easy to handle. On a lightly floured surface, roll out to 1/4-in. thickness. Cut with 2-1/2-in. cookie cutters dipped in flour. Place 1 in. apart on ungreased baking sheets. Bake at 350° for 8-10 minutes or until edges are firm. Remove to wire racks to cool. For frosting, combine water and gelatin in a saucepan; let stand for 5 minutes to soften. Stir in sugar; bring to a boil. Reduce heat; simmer for 10 minutes. Remove from the heat; stir in confectioners' sugar. Transfer to a mixing bowl; beat until foamy. Add baking powder and vanilla; beat on high until for 5-8 minutes or until thick. Frost cookies. Let dry on wire racks. **Yield:** about 4-1/2 dozen.

Chewy Tangerine Cookies

Janyce Barstad, Anchorage, Alaska

This recipe represents my Scandinavian heritage. The blend of spices and hint of tangerine have made these cookies a favorite to serve with a mug of hot coffee.

>   1/2 cup butter (no substitutes), softened
>   1/2 cup sugar
>   1/2 cup dark corn syrup
>   1 egg
>   1 tablespoon grated tangerine *or* orange peel
> 2-1/4 cups all-purpose flour
>   1/2 teaspoon baking soda
>   1/2 teaspoon ground cloves
>   1/2 teaspoon ground nutmeg
>   1/4 teaspoon salt

In a mixing bowl, cream butter and sugar. In a small saucepan, bring corn syrup to a boil; gradually add to the creamed mixture. Beat in egg and tangerine peel. Combine flour, baking soda, cloves, nutmeg and salt; gradually add to the creamed mixture. Cover and refrigerate for 2 hours or until easy to handle. On a lightly floured surface, roll out to 1/4-in. thickness. Cut with 2-1/2-in. cookie cutters dipped in flour. Place 1 in. apart on greased baking sheets. Bake at 375° for 8-10 minutes or until edges are firm. Remove to wire racks to cool. **Yield:** about 3 dozen.

Buttery Walnut Cutouts

Grace Simons, Orange City, Florida

Chopped walnuts add flavor and crunch to a typical butter cookie plus give them a pretty golden color.

>   1 cup butter (no substitutes), softened
>   3/4 cup sugar
>   1 egg
>   1 teaspoon vanilla extract
> 2-1/2 cups all-purpose flour

Cutout Classics

2 teaspoons baking powder
1/2 teaspoon salt
1 cup chopped walnuts

In a mixing bowl, cream butter and sugar. Beat in egg and vanilla. Combine flour, baking powder and salt; gradually add to the creamed mixture. Stir in walnuts. Cover and refrigerate for 1 hour or until easy to handle. On a floured surface, roll out to 1/8-in. thickness. Cut with 2-in. cookie cutters dipped in flour. Place 1 in. apart on ungreased baking sheets. Bake at 375° for 6-8 minutes or until edges are golden brown. Remove to wire racks to cool. **Yield:** 4 dozen.

Swedish Spice Cutouts

Lilly Decker, Clancy, Montana

My sister, Judith Landgren of White Sulphur Springs, Montana, brought this recipe with her when she came to the United States from Sweden in 1928.

1-1/2 cups butter (no substitutes), softened
1-3/4 cups packed dark brown sugar
1 egg
2/3 cup dark corn syrup
1/4 cup molasses
4-1/2 cups all-purpose flour
1-1/4 teaspoons ground cinnamon
1 teaspoon baking soda
3/4 teaspoon ground cloves
Slivered almonds, optional

In a mixing bowl, cream butter and brown sugar. Beat in egg, corn syrup and molasses. Combine flour, cinnamon, baking soda and cloves; gradually add to creamed mixture. Cover and refrigerate for 4 hours or until easy to handle. On a lightly floured surface, roll out to 1/8-in. thickness. Cut with 2-1/2-in. cookie cutters dipped in flour. Place 1 in. apart on ungreased baking sheets. Top with almonds if desired. Bake at 375° for 8-10 minutes or until edges are lightly browned. Remove to wire racks to cool. **Yield:** about 10 dozen.

Lemon Sugar Cookies

Vivian Hines, New Philadelphia, Ohio

These light cookies are crisp on the outside and soft inside, making it hard to eat just one! I most often bake them for Christmas and Valentine's Day.

2 cups butter *or* margarine, softened
4 cups confectioners' sugar
4 eggs
3 tablespoons lemon juice
3 tablespoons half-and-half cream

2 teaspoons grated lemon peel
6-1/2 cups all-purpose flour
1 teaspoon baking soda
1/4 teaspoon salt
Sugar

In a mixing bowl, cream butter and confectioners' sugar. Add the eggs, one at a time, beating well after each addition. Beat in lemon juice, cream and lemon peel. Combine flour, baking soda and salt; gradually add to the creamed mixture. Cover and refrigerate for 2 hours or until easy to handle. On a lightly floured surface, roll out to 1/8-in. thickness. Cut with 2-1/2-in. cookie cutters dipped in flour. Place 1 in. apart on ungreased baking sheets. Sprinkle with sugar. Bake at 350° for 8-10 minutes or until lightly browned. Remove to wire racks to cool. **Yield:** about 13 dozen.

Orange Sugar Rollouts

Margaret Hancock, Camp Verde, Arizona

When my children were young, we would bake and decorate these cookies every Christmas. Now I carry on the tradition with my grandchildren.

2/3 cup shortening
3/4 cup sugar
1/2 to 1 teaspoon grated orange peel
1 egg
4 teaspoons milk
1/2 teaspoon vanilla extract
2 cups all-purpose flour
1-1/2 teaspoons baking powder
1/4 teaspoon salt
FROSTING:
1/2 cup butter *or* margarine, softened
4 cups confectioners' sugar
1 teaspoon vanilla extract
1/2 teaspoon grated orange peel
2 to 4 tablespoons orange juice
Yellow food coloring, optional

In a mixing bowl, cream shortening, sugar and orange peel. Beat in egg, milk and vanilla. Combine flour, baking powder and salt; gradually add to the creamed mixture. On a lightly floured surface, roll out to 1/4-in. thickness. Cut with 2-1/2-in. cookie cutters dipped in flour. Place 1 in. apart on greased baking sheets. Bake at 375° for 6-8 minutes or until lightly browned. Remove to wire racks to cool. In a mixing bowl, combine butter, confectioners' sugar, vanilla, orange peel and enough orange juice to achieve spreading consistency. Add food coloring if desired. Frost cookies. **Yield:** about 3-1/2 dozen. **Editor's Note:** Instead of rolling and cutting out these cookies, the dough may be dropped by tablespoonfuls onto greased baking sheets. Bake and frost as directed.

Chocolate Oatmeal Stars

Edna Hall, Aitkin, Minnesota

Fans of oatmeal cookies will love this variation that combines oats, chocolate and coconut. These star-shaped cookies "shine" wherever I take them!

2/3 cup shortening
1 cup sugar
1 egg
1 teaspoon vanilla extract
1/2 teaspoon almond extract
1 cup (6 ounces) semisweet chocolate chips, melted
1 cup all-purpose flour
1 teaspoon salt
1/2 teaspoon baking soda
1 cup quick-cooking oats
1 cup flaked coconut, finely chopped
Colored sugar *or* nonpareils

In a mixing bowl, cream shortening and sugar. Beat in egg and extracts. Stir in melted chocolate chips. Combine flour, salt and baking soda; gradually add to the creamed mixture. Stir in oats and coconut. Cover and refrigerate for 2 hours or until easy to handle. On a lightly floured surface, roll out to 1/8-in. thickness. Cut with a 3-in. star-shaped cookie cutter dipped in flour. Place 1 in. apart on ungreased baking sheets. Sprinkle with colored sugar or nonpareils. Bake at 350° for 7-9 minutes or until firm. Remove to wire racks to cool. **Yield:** about 3 dozen.

Maple Sugar Cookies

Anna Glaus, Greensburg, Pennsylvania

This recipe is requested by friends and family every time I'm asked to bring cookies for an event. Folks enjoy the subtle maple flavor in this crisp cookie.

1 cup butter-flavored shortening
1-1/4 cups sugar
2 eggs
1/4 cup maple syrup
1 tablespoon vanilla extract
3 cups all-purpose flour
3/4 teaspoon baking powder
1/2 teaspoon baking soda
1/2 teaspoon salt

In a mixing bowl, cream shortening and sugar. Add eggs, one at a time, beating well after each addition. Beat in syrup and vanilla. Combine the remaining ingredients; gradually add to the creamed mixture.

Cover and refrigerate for 2 hours or until easy to handle. On a lightly floured surface, roll out to 1/8-in. thickness. Cut with 2-1/2-in. cookie cutters dipped in flour. Place 1 in. apart on ungreased baking sheets. Bake at 375° for 8-10 minutes or until golden brown. Remove to wire racks to cool. **Yield:** 4 dozen.

Lemon Leaves

Karen Minthorne, Rancho Cucamonga, California

Sugar, chopped pistachios and lemon peel sprinkled on top of these cookies make them extra special. Feel free to use whatever cookie cutters you have on hand.

1/2 cup butter (no substitutes), softened
1-1/3 cups sugar, *divided*
1 egg
1 tablespoon half-and-half cream
1 teaspoon lemon extract
2-1/4 cups all-purpose flour
3 teaspoons baking powder
1/2 teaspoon salt
2 egg yolks
1 teaspoon water
1/4 cup finely chopped pistachios
1-1/2 teaspoons grated lemon peel

In a mixing bowl, cream butter and 1 cup of sugar. Beat in egg, cream and extract. Combine flour, baking powder and salt; gradually add to the creamed mixture. Cover and refrigerate for 2 hours or until easy to handle. In a small bowl, beat egg yolks and water. In another bowl, combine pistachios, lemon peel and remaining sugar. On a lightly floured surface, roll out dough to 1/8-in. thickness. Cut with a 2-1/2-in. leaf-shaped cookie cutter dipped in flour. Place 1 in. apart on ungreased baking sheets. Brush with egg yolk mixture; sprinkle with pistachio mixture. Bake at 350° for 6-8 minutes or until edges are set (do not brown). Remove to wire racks to cool. **Yield:** about 4-1/2 dozen.

Apricot-Filled Triangles

Mildred Lorence, Carlisle, Pennsylvania

I'm an avid cookie baker, so I'm always trying new recipes on the family. These lovely looking cookies are perfect when you want to offer friends and family something a little more special.

1 pound dried apricots (2-1/2 cups)
1-1/2 cups water
1/2 cup sugar

DOUGH:
  2/3 cup shortening
  3 tablespoons milk
1-1/3 cups sugar
  2 eggs
  1 teaspoon lemon extract
  4 cups cake flour
  2 teaspoons baking powder
  1 teaspoon salt

In a saucepan, cook the apricots and water over low heat for 45 minutes or until until the water is absorbed and apricots are soft. Cool slightly; transfer to a blender or food processor. Cover and process until smooth. Add sugar; cover and process until blended. Set aside. In a large saucepan over low heat, melt shortening and milk. Remove from the heat; stir in sugar. Add eggs, one at a time, whisking well after each addition. Stir in extract. Combine flour, baking powder and salt; gradually add to the saucepan. Cover and refrigerate for 4 hours or until easy to handle. On a lightly floured surface, roll out to 1/8-in. thickness. Cut with a 3-in. round cookie cutter dipped in flour. Place 1 teaspoon apricot filling in the center of each. Bring three edges together over filling, overlapping slightly (a small portion of filling will show in the center); pinch edges gently. Place 1 in. apart on ungreased baking sheets. Bake at 400° for 8-10 minutes or until golden brown. Remove to wire racks to cool. **Yield:** 6 dozen.

Buttery Sugar Cookies

Cynthia Olson, Springfield, Illinois

It's a good thing this recipe makes a big batch because no one can stop eating just one! These crisp buttery cookies truly do melt in your mouth.

  2 cups butter (no substitutes), softened
  2 cups sugar
  3 eggs
  5 tablespoons milk
  1 teaspoon vanilla extract
6-1/2 cups all-purpose flour
  1 teaspoon baking soda
  1 teaspoon baking powder
  1 teaspoon salt
Additional sugar
Walnut halves *or* raisins, optional

In a mixing bowl, cream butter and sugar. Add eggs, one at a time, beating well after each addition. Beat in milk and vanilla. Combine the flour, baking soda, baking powder and salt; gradually add to the creamed mixture. Cover and refrigerate for 1 hour or until easy to handle. On a lightly floured surface, roll out to 1/4-in. thickness. Cut with 2-1/2-in. cookie cutters dipped in flour. Place 1 in. apart on greased baking sheets. Sprinkle with sugar; place a walnut or raisin in the center of each if desired. Bake at 350° for 8-10 minutes or until lightly browned. Remove to wire racks to cool. **Yield:** about 11-1/2 dozen.

Vanilla Butter Rollouts

Colleen Sickman, Charles City, Iowa

Even cooks who normally shy away from rolled cookies can make these with confidence. The dough is so easy to work with after a mere 30 minutes of chilling.

1-1/2 cups butter (no substitutes), softened
1-1/2 cups sugar
  2 eggs
  1 tablespoon vanilla extract
  4 cups all-purpose flour
  1 teaspoon baking soda
  1 teaspoon cream of tartar
  1 teaspoon salt
FROSTING:
  6 tablespoons butter (no substitutes), softened
  3 cups confectioners' sugar
1/4 cup milk
  1 tablespoon vanilla extract
Colored sugar, optional

In a mixing bowl, cream butter and sugar. Add eggs, one at a time, beating well after each addition. Beat in vanilla. Combine flour, baking soda, cream of tartar and salt; gradually add to the creamed mixture. Cover and refrigerate for 30 minutes or until easy to handle. On a lightly floured surface, roll out to 1/4-in. thickness. Cut with 2-1/2-in. cookie cutters dipped in flour. Place 2 in. apart on ungreased baking sheets. Bake at 350° for 8-10 minutes or until lightly browned. For frosting, combine butter, confectioners' sugar, milk and vanilla in a mixing bowl; beat until smooth. Spread or drizzle over cookies. Sprinkle with colored sugar if desired. **Yield:** about 7 dozen.

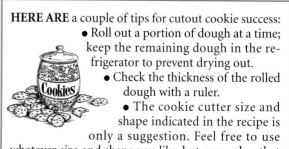

HERE ARE a couple of tips for cutout cookie success:
 • Roll out a portion of dough at a time; keep the remaining dough in the refrigerator to prevent drying out.
 • Check the thickness of the rolled dough with a ruler.
 • The cookie cutter size and shape indicated in the recipe is only a suggestion. Feel free to use whatever size and shape you like, but remember that may affect the yield.

Shaped Specialties

Dutch Treats

Ava Rexrode, Blue Grass, Virginia

(Pictured at left)

I was born and raised in Holland, where we used almond paste quite often in our baking. I created this recipe to capture the outstanding flavors of home.

> 1 cup butter (no substitutes), softened
> 2 packages (3 ounces *each*) cream cheese, softened
> 2 cups all-purpose flour

FILLING:

> 3 eggs
> 1 cup sugar
> 1 can (8 ounces) almond paste, cut into cubes

Sliced almonds

In a mixing bowl, cream butter and cream cheese. Gradually add the flour. Cover and refrigerate for 1 hour or until easy to handle. Roll into 1-in. balls. Press dough onto the bottom and up the sides of ungreased miniature muffin cups; set aside. For filling, beat eggs in a mixing bowl until light and fluffy. Add sugar; mix well. Beat in the almond paste. Spoon a rounded teaspoonful into each cup; top each with three almond slices. Bake at 325° for 25-30 minutes or until lightly browned and filling is set. Cool for 10 minutes before removing to wire racks. **Yield:** about 10 dozen.

Cream Cheese Bells

Charlene Grimminger, Paris, Ohio

(Pictured at left)

Since I was raised on a dairy farm, the ingredients in this recipe suit me fine! These delicious cookies freeze well, although most of them get gobbled up before I have a chance to get them in the freezer.

> 7 tablespoons butter (no substitutes), softened

TEATIME SWEETS. Pictured at left, top to bottom: Cream Cheese Bells, Dutch Treats and Almond-Tipped Shortbread Fingers (all recipes on this page).

> 1 package (8 ounces) cream cheese, softened
> 2 egg yolks
> 2-1/2 cups all-purpose flour

FILLING:

> 2-1/2 cups ground pecans *or* walnuts
> 1/2 cup sugar
> 1/4 cup butter (no substitutes), melted
> 1 egg white

Confectioners' sugar

In a mixing bowl, cream butter and cream cheese. Beat in egg yolks. Gradually add flour. Cover and refrigerate overnight. Remove from refrigerator about 1 hour before rolling. For filling, combine the nuts, sugar, butter and egg white; set aside. Divide dough into fourths. On a floured surface, roll out each portion to 1/8-in. thickness. Cut with a 2-3/4-in. round cookie cutter. Place 1 in. apart on ungreased baking sheets. Place 1 teaspoon filling in center of each circle. Shape into a cone by folding edges of dough to meet over filling. Moisten edges with water and pinch edges together. Bake at 350° for 12-15 minutes or until lightly browned. Roll warm cookies in confectioners' sugar; cool on wire racks. **Yield:** about 4 dozen. **Editor's Note:** If bells open during baking, gently press together with a fork while warm.

Almond-Tipped Shortbread Fingers

Cindy Sifford, Mt. Zion, Illinois

(Pictured at left)

My husband enjoys these cookies so much that he usually can't wait until they're set to start eating them. If you'd like, try dipping them into melted semisweet chocolate and chopped pecans.

> 1 cup butter (no substitutes), softened
> 3/4 cup packed brown sugar
> 2 teaspoons vanilla extract
> 2 cups all-purpose flour
> 6 squares (1 ounce *each*) white baking chocolate

1-1/4 cups chopped almonds

In a mixing bowl, cream butter and brown sugar. Beat in vanilla. Gradually add flour. Shape 1/2 cupfuls of dough into 1/2-in.-thick logs. Cut logs into 2-in. pieces. Place 2 in. apart on ungreased baking sheets. Bake at 325° for 15-17 minutes or until lightly browned. Remove to wire racks to cool. In a microwave or double boiler, melt chocolate. Dip one end of each cookie into chocolate, then into almonds. Place on waxed paper to harden. **Yield:** 4 dozen.

English Tea Cakes

Beverly Christian, Fort Worth, Texas

These unique cookies are baked in muffin cups, giving them a perfectly round shape. I sometimes omit the pecans and decorate the cookies for holidays.

> **2 cups butter (no substitutes), softened**
> **1 cup sugar**
> **2 teaspoons vanilla extract**
> **4 cups all-purpose flour**
> **60 pecan halves**

In a mixing bowl, cream butter and sugar. Beat in vanilla. Gradually add flour. Drop by heaping tablespoonfuls into greased muffin cups; flatten slightly. Press a pecan half in the center of each. Bake at 350° for 10-12 minutes or until edges are lightly browned. Cool for 2 minutes in pans. Invert pans to remove. Place pecan side up on wire racks to cool completely. **Yield:** 5 dozen.

Fancy Peanut Butter Cookies

Janet Hooper, Emporium, Pennsylvania

I always received compliments on my moist and chewy peanut butter cookies. But I wondered how to make them even more special, and I decided to decorate them!

> **1 cup shortening**
> **1 cup peanut butter**
> **1 cup sugar**
> **1 cup packed brown sugar**
> **2 eggs**
> **1/4 cup milk**
> **2 teaspoons vanilla extract**
> **3-1/2 cups all-purpose flour**
> **2 teaspoons baking soda**
> **1 teaspoon salt**
> **FROSTING:**
> **1/4 cup butter *or* margarine, softened**
> **1/4 cup shortening**
> **1/4 cup peanut butter**
> **4 cups confectioners' sugar**
> **1/4 cup milk**
> **1 teaspoon vanilla extract**
> **Pinch salt**
> **ICING:**
> **1/2 cup semisweet chocolate chips, melted**
> **2 tablespoons milk**

In a mixing bowl, cream shortening, peanut butter and sugars. Add eggs, one at a time, beating well after each addition. Beat in milk and vanilla. Combine flour, baking soda and salt; gradually add to the creamed mixture. Roll into 1-in. balls. Place 2 in. apart on ungreased baking sheets. Bake at 375° for 10-12 minutes or until golden brown. Remove to wire racks. For frosting, cream butter, shortening, peanut butter and confectioners' sugar in a mixing bowl. Beat in milk, vanilla and salt until smooth. Frost cooled cookies. Combine icing ingredients; drizzle over frosting. **Yield:** 7-1/2 dozen.

Lemon Dreams

Karen Scaglione, Nanuet, New York

A buttery cookie with a luscious lemon filling is simply hard to resist. Every time I serve these elegant cookies, I'm asked for the recipe.

> **1 cup butter (no substitutes), softened**
> **1/3 cup confectioners' sugar**
> **1 teaspoon vanilla extract**
> **1-2/3 cups all-purpose flour**
> **FILLING:**
> **2/3 cup sugar**
> **1-1/2 teaspoons cornstarch**
> **1 teaspoon grated lemon peel**
> **1/4 teaspoon salt**
> **1 egg, beaten**
> **3 tablespoons lemon juice**
> **1 tablespoon butter *or* margarine, melted**
> **Confectioners' sugar, optional**

In a mixing bowl, cream butter and confectioners' sugar. Beat in vanilla. Gradually add flour. Cover and refrigerate for 30 minutes or until easy to handle. Roll into 1-in. balls. Place 2 in. apart on ungreased baking sheets. Using the end of a wooden spoon handle, make an indentation in the center of each. Bake at 350° for 12-14 minutes or until lightly browned. Remove to wire racks to cool. For filling, combine the sugar, cornstarch, lemon peel and salt in a saucepan. Stir in egg, lemon juice and butter until smooth. Cook over medium-high heat until thickened. Reduce heat; cook and stir 2 minutes longer. Cool. Spoon 1/2 teaspoonful into each cookie. Dust with confectioners' sugar if desired. **Yield:** 3 dozen.

Macaroon Kisses

Angie Lansman, Perry, Iowa

One taste and I think you'll agree this is the best coconut cookie you've ever tasted. These eye-catching cookies are always the first to disappear from the cookie tray.

> **1/3 cup butter *or* margarine, softened**
> **1 package (3 ounces) cream cheese, softened**

3/4 cup sugar
1 egg yolk
2 teaspoons orange juice
2 teaspoons almond extract
1-1/4 cups all-purpose flour
2 teaspoons baking powder
1/4 teaspoon salt
1 package (14 ounces) flaked coconut, *divided*
1 package (13 ounces) milk chocolate kisses

In a mixing bowl, cream butter, cream cheese and sugar. Beat in egg yolk, orange juice and extract. Combine flour, baking powder and salt; gradually add to the creamed mixture. Stir in 3-2/3 cups coconut. Cover and refrigerate for 30 minutes or until easy to handle. Roll into 1-in. balls, then roll in remaining coconut. Place 1 in. apart on ungreased baking sheets. Bake at 350° for 12-15 minutes or until the edges are lightly browned. Immediately press a chocolate kiss into the center of each cookie. Cool for 1 minute before removing to wire racks. **Yield:** about 4-1/2 dozen.

Crispy Scotchies

Joanne Kramer, Manchester, Iowa

I first tasted these cookies as a newlywed in 1959. Over the years, I've made a few modifications, and now they turn out perfectly every time.

6 tablespoons butter *or* margarine, softened
6 tablespoons butter-flavored shortening
1 cup sugar
1 cup packed brown sugar
2 eggs
1 teaspoon vanilla extract
4 cups crisp rice cereal, *divided*
1-1/2 cups all-purpose flour
1 teaspoon baking soda
1/2 teaspoon baking powder
1 cup butterscotch chips
TOPPING:
1/2 cup sugar
1/2 cup packed brown sugar

In a mixing bowl, cream butter, shortening and sugars. Add eggs, one at a time, beating well after each addition. Beat in vanilla. Crush 2 cups of cereal; add flour, baking soda and baking powder. Gradually add to the creamed mixture. Stir in butterscotch chips and remaining cereal. Combine topping ingredients in a small bowl. Roll dough into 1-1/4-in. balls, then roll in topping. Place 2 in. apart on ungreased baking sheets; flatten slightly with a glass. Bake at 350° for 10-12 minutes or until golden brown. Cool for 1 minute before removing to wire racks. **Yield:** about 5-1/2 dozen.

Crunchy Whole Wheat Cookies

Miranda Hilgers, Madison Lake, Minnesota

One day, my grandmother and I were planning on making cookies, but she didn't have all-purpose flour. I suggested we use whole wheat flour. The result is a crisp hearty cookie loaded with flavor.

2/3 cup butter *or* margarine, softened
2/3 cup shortening
1 cup sugar
1 cup packed brown sugar
2 eggs
2 teaspoons vanilla extract
3-1/2 cups whole wheat flour
1 teaspoon baking soda

In a mixing bowl, cream butter, shortening and sugars. Add eggs, one at a time, beating well after each addition. Beat in vanilla. Combine flour and baking soda; gradually add to creamed mixture. Roll into 1-in. balls. Place 2 in. apart on greased baking sheets. Flatten with a glass dipped in sugar. Bake at 375° for 10-12 minutes or until golden brown. Remove to wire racks to cool. **Yield:** about 6-1/2 dozen.

Yummy Pecan Bites

Alice Marie Puckett, Spokane, Washington

After experimenting with different recipes and ingredients, I came up with this simply delicious recipe that's reminiscent of the ever-popular Snickerdoodle.

1 cup shortening
1-1/2 cups sugar
2 eggs
2-3/4 cups all-purpose flour
2 teaspoons cream of tartar
1 teaspoon baking soda
1/4 teaspoon salt
1 cup finely chopped pecans
TOPPING:
3 tablespoons sugar
1-1/2 teaspoons ground cinnamon

In a mixing bowl, cream shortening and sugar. Add eggs, one at a time, beating well after each addition. Combine the flour, cream of tartar, baking soda and salt; gradually add to creamed mixture. Stir in pecans. Combine topping ingredients in a small bowl. Roll dough into 1-in. balls, then roll in topping. Place 2 in. apart on ungreased baking sheets; flatten slightly. Bake at 400° for 10-12 minutes or until surface cracks. Remove to wire racks to cool. **Yield:** 5 dozen.

Butter Crunch Cookies

Monique Swallow, Corpus Christi, Texas

I've given this recipe to more people than any other recipe I have. These cookies are so easy to make. Cornflakes and pecans give them their delightful crunch.

> 2 cups butter (no substitutes), softened
> 2 cups sugar
> 3 cups all-purpose flour
> 2 teaspoons cream of tartar
> 2 teaspoons baking soda
> 1/2 teaspoon salt
> 4 cups cornflakes, lightly crushed
> 1 cup chopped pecans

In a mixing bowl, cream butter and sugar. Combine flour, cream of tartar, baking soda and salt; gradually add to the creamed mixture. Stir in the cornflakes and pecans. Roll into 1-in. balls. Place 1 in. apart on ungreased baking sheets. Bake at 350° for 10-12 minutes or until lightly browned. Cool for 2 minutes before removing to wire racks. **Yield:** about 8 dozen.

Calypso Cups

Mrs. Frank Kaczmarek, Steubenville, Ohio

These are great cookies to prepare for parties throughout the year. I simply tint the frosting for the occasion—red for Valentine's Day, pastel colors for baby showers and green for Christmas.

> 1 cup butter (no substitutes), softened
> 2 packages (3 ounces *each*) cream cheese, softened
> 2 cups all-purpose flour
> FILLING:
> 1/2 cup flaked coconut
> 1/2 cup sugar
> 1-1/2 teaspoons cornstarch
> 1 can (8 ounces) crushed pineapple, undrained
> 1 egg
> FROSTING:
> 2 cups confectioners' sugar
> 1/2 cup shortening
> 1 teaspoon vanilla extract
> 3 to 4 tablespoons milk
> Additional flaked coconut
> 3/4 cup finely chopped walnuts

In a mixing bowl, cream butter and cream cheese. Gradually add flour. Cover and refrigerate for 1 hour or until easy to handle. Roll into 1-in. balls. Press onto the bottom and up the sides of greased minia-

ture muffin cups. Combine filling ingredients; spoon into cups. Bake at 350° for 15-20 minutes or until edges are lightly browned. Cool in pans on wire racks. For frosting, combine the sugar, shortening and vanilla; add enough milk to achieve spreading consistency. Remove cooled cups from pans; top each with a pinch of coconut. Frost and sprinkle with walnuts. **Yield:** 4 dozen.

Chocolate-Filled Poppy Seed Cookies

Karen Mead, Granville, New York

While it's been around for years, this recipe remains enjoyable to this day. A co-worker prepared these at a cookie exchange a while back…they were the biggest hit of the party.

> 1 cup butter (no substitutes), softened
> 1/2 cup sugar
> 2 egg yolks
> 1 teaspoon vanilla extract
> 2 cups all-purpose flour
> 3 tablespoons poppy seeds
> 1/4 teaspoon salt
> 1 cup (6 ounces) semisweet chocolate chips, melted

In a mixing bowl, cream butter and sugar. Beat in egg yolks and vanilla. Combine flour, poppy seeds and salt; gradually add to the creamed mixture. Roll into 1-in. balls. Place 2 in. apart on ungreased baking sheets. Using the end of a wooden spoon handle, make an indentation in the center of each. Bake at 375° for 10-12 minutes or until lightly browned. Immediately make an indentation in the center again. Remove to wire racks to cool slightly; fill with melted chocolate. **Yield:** 6-1/2 dozen.

Double Chocolate Treats

Tracy Lynn Ware, Saginaw, Michigan

This recipe is for me because I can't get enough chocolate! I like to make these tasty cookies for my family.

> 1 cup butter (no substitutes), softened
> 1 cup sugar
> 1 cup packed brown sugar
> 2 eggs
> 1/2 cup light corn syrup
> 1 teaspoon vanilla extract
> 4 cups all-purpose flour
> 1/2 cup plus 1 tablespoon baking cocoa
> 2 teaspoons baking soda

1/2 teaspoon salt
3 cups milk chocolate chips
Additional sugar, optional

In a mixing bowl, cream butter and sugars. Add the eggs, one at a time, beating well after each addition. Beat in corn syrup and vanilla. Combine flour, cocoa, baking soda and salt; gradually add to the creamed mixture. Stir in chocolate chips. Roll into 1-1/2-in. balls; roll in sugar if desired. Place 2 in. apart on ungreased baking sheets. Bake at 350° for 12-14 minutes or until cracks look dry. Cool for 2 minutes before removing to wire racks. **Yield:** 5 dozen.

Secret Ginger Cookies

Hazel Porter, Sublimity, Oregon

White pepper and ground mustard are the secret ingredients in this recipe. My sons can't stop eating these slightly spicy chewy cookies.

3/4 cup shortening
1 cup packed brown sugar
1/4 cup molasses
1 egg
2-1/4 cups all-purpose flour
2 teaspoons baking soda
2 teaspoons ground ginger
1 teaspoon ground cinnamon
1/2 teaspoon *each* ground white pepper, mustard and cardamom
1/4 teaspoon salt
1/4 teaspoon ground cloves
Additional sugar

In a mixing bowl, cream shortening and brown sugar. Beat in molasses and egg. Combine flour, baking soda, ginger, cinnamon, pepper, mustard, cardamom, salt and cloves; gradually add to the creamed mixture. Cover and refrigerate for 1 hour or until easy to handle. Roll into 1-in. balls, then roll in sugar. Bake at 375° for 10-12 minutes or until surface cracks. Remove to wire racks to cool. **Yield:** 4-1/2 dozen.

Special Oatmeal Chip Cookies

Carol Poskie, Pittsburgh, Pennsylvania

My son dubbed these "the cookie" after just one taste, and they've become my signature cookie since then. I haven't shared my "secret" recipe until now.

1 cup butter *or* margarine, softened
1 cup peanut butter
1 cup sugar
1 cup packed brown sugar

2 eggs
1 teaspoon vanilla extract
3 cups old-fashioned oats
1 cup all-purpose flour
2 teaspoons ground cinnamon
1 teaspoon baking soda
1/4 teaspoon ground nutmeg
1-1/2 cups semisweet chocolate chips
DRIZZLE:
1 cup white chocolate confectionary coating,* melted
1 cup dark chocolate confectionary coating,* melted

In a mixing bowl, cream butter, peanut butter and sugars. Add eggs, one at a time, beating well after each addition. Beat in vanilla. Combine oats, flour, cinnamon, baking soda and nutmeg; gradually add to the creamed mixture. Stir in chocolate chips. Roll into 1-in. balls. Place 2 in. apart on greased baking sheets; flatten to 1/2-in. thickness. Bake at 350° for 10-12 minutes or until golden brown. Remove to wire racks to cool. Drizzle with white coating in one direction, then with dark coating in the opposite direction to form a crisscross pattern. **Yield:** about 5-1/2 dozen. ***Editor's Note:** Confectionary coating is found in the baking section of most grocery stores. It is sometimes labeled "almond bark" or "candy coating" and is often sold in bulk packages of 1 to 1-1/2 pounds.

Crisp Almond Cookies

Nelson Rauschkolb, Venice, Florida

I found this recipe in a magazine years ago and have shared it with family and friends many times since. These slightly sweet crisp cookies bring a flavorful ending to any meal.

1/2 cup butter (no substitutes), softened
1/2 cup shortening
1 cup confectioners' sugar
1 tablespoon water
1 teaspoon vanilla extract
2 cups all-purpose flour
1/2 teaspoon salt
1 cup finely chopped almonds
Additional confectioners' sugar

In a mixing bowl, cream butter, shortening and sugar. Beat in water and vanilla. Combine flour and salt; gradually add to the creamed mixture. Stir in almonds. Roll into 1-in. balls. Place 2 in. apart on ungreased baking sheets; flatten slightly with a fork. Bake at 350° for 12-14 minutes or until lightly browned. Remove to wire racks to cool. Dust with confectioners' sugar. **Yield:** 5 dozen.

Brown Sugar Cookies

Leonora Cloon, Ironwood, Michigan

I received this recipe some 40 years ago at a shower where the hostess asked each guest to share a favorite recipe. This was the most popular of them all. Dark brown sugar gives these cookies added richness.

  1 cup butter (no substitutes), **softened**
  3/4 cup sugar, *divided*
  1/2 cup packed dark brown sugar
  1 egg
  1 teaspoon vanilla extract
  2 cups all-purpose flour
  1/2 cup finely ground pecans
  1 teaspoon salt
  1/2 teaspoon baking soda
ICING:
  1 cup packed dark brown sugar
  1/2 cup half-and-half cream
  1 cup confectioners' sugar

In a mixing bowl, cream butter, 1/2 cup sugar and brown sugar. Beat in egg and vanilla. Combine the flour, pecans, salt and baking soda; gradually add to creamed mixture. Cover and refrigerate for 20 minutes or until easy to handle. Roll into 1-in. balls, then roll in remaining sugar. Place 2 in. apart on ungreased baking sheets. Flatten with a glass dipped in sugar. Bake at 350° for 10-12 minutes or until edges are lightly browned. Remove to wire racks to cool. For icing, combine brown sugar and cream in a saucepan. Bring to a boil; boil and stir for 4 minutes. Remove from the heat. Sift confectioners' sugar into the hot mixture; stir until combined. Drizzle icing over cookies. **Yield:** 5-1/2 dozen.

Pecan Fingers

Irene Risbry, Colorado Springs, Colorado

You can't go wrong with the combination of butter and pecans in this recipe. I never serve these cookies without receiving requests for it.

  1 cup butter (no substitutes), **softened**
  1/2 cup confectioners' sugar
  2 cups all-purpose flour
  1/2 teaspoon salt
  1 cup finely chopped pecans
Additional confectioners' sugar

In a mixing bowl, cream butter and sugar. Combine flour and salt; gradually add to creamed mixture. Stir in pecans. Shape tablespoonfuls into 2-in. fingers.

Place 2 in. apart on ungreased baking sheets. Bake at 350° for 15-18 minutes or until lightly browned. Roll warm cookies in confectioners' sugar; cool on wire racks. **Yield:** about 4 dozen.

Sugared Cherry Jewels

Jennifer Branum, O'Fallon, Illinois

The texture and crunch of the sugar coating make these chewy cookies extra special. I love the bright cherry center and the fact that they look lovely in a holiday gift box or tin.

  1 cup butter (no substitutes), **softened**
  1/2 cup sugar
  1/3 cup light corn syrup
  2 eggs, *separated*
  1/2 teaspoon vanilla extract
2-1/2 cups all-purpose flour
Additional sugar
  1 jar (10 ounces) maraschino cherries, **drained and halved**

In a mixing bowl, cream butter and sugar. Beat in corn syrup, egg yolks and vanilla. Gradually add the flour. Cover and refrigerate for 1 hour or until easy to handle. Roll into 1-in. balls. Beat egg whites until foamy; roll balls in egg whites, then in sugar. Place 2 in. apart on ungreased baking sheets. Using the end of a wooden spoon handle, make an indentation in the center of each. Press a cherry half in the center. Bake at 325° for 14-16 minutes or until lightly browned. Remove to wire racks to cool. **Yield:** about 5 dozen.

Caramel Pecan Treasures

Glenda MacEachern, Crown Point, Indiana

Fancy-looking cookies like these may take some time to prepare, but family and friends will surely be impressed! No one can resist the shortbread cookie, caramel filling and melted chocolate top sprinkled with pecans.

  1 cup butter (no substitutes), **softened**
  3/4 cup packed brown sugar
  1 teaspoon vanilla extract
1-3/4 cups all-purpose flour
  1/2 teaspoon baking powder
  30 caramels, halved and flattened
  2 cups (12 ounces) semisweet chocolate chips
  1 tablespoon shortening
  1/2 cup finely chopped pecans

In a mixing bowl, cream butter and brown sugar. Beat in vanilla. Combine the flour and baking powder; gradually add to the creamed mixture. Roll into 1-in. balls. Place 2 in. apart on baking sheets; flatten slightly. Bake at 325° for 12-15 minutes or until golden brown. Remove to wire racks to cool. Place one caramel on each cooled cookie. Melt the chocolate chips and shortening; spread over cookies. Sprinkle with pecans. Let stand until firm. **Yield:** 5 dozen.

Chocolate Macadamia Meltaways

Barbara Sepcich, Galt, California

I came up with this recipe by accident one day when I wanted to make some cookies. I decided to use some ingredients already in my cupboard, and these were the delicious result.

> 1/2 cup butter (no substitutes), softened
> 1/4 cup confectioners' sugar
> 1/2 teaspoon vanilla extract
> 1-1/4 cups all-purpose flour
> 1 jar (3-1/2 ounces) macadamia nuts, finely chopped
> **FILLING:**
> 1 cup (6 ounces) semisweet chocolate chips
> 1/2 cup coarsely chopped macadamia nuts
> **Additional confectioners' sugar**

In a mixing bowl, cream butter and sugar. Beat in vanilla. Gradually add flour. Stir in nuts (dough will be stiff); set aside. For filling, melt chocolate chips. Stir in nuts; cool slightly. Drop by 1/2 teaspoonfuls onto a waxed paper-lined baking sheet; cover and refrigerate for 30 minutes. Shape teaspoonfuls of dough around each piece of chocolate-nut mixture so it is completely covered. Place 2 in. apart on ungreased baking sheets. Bake at 375° for 12-14 minutes or until lightly browned. Roll warm cookies in confectioners' sugar; cool on wire racks. **Yield:** 2-1/2 dozen.

No-Bake Strawberry Cookies

Mrs. V. Ferraiuolo, Bedford Heights, Ohio

These no-bake date and crisp rice cereal cookies are shaped into "strawberries" and topped with a colorful "stem". Serve them when you want to offer something fun and different.

> 1 package (8 ounces) chopped dates
> 1/2 cup flaked coconut
> 1/2 cup sugar
> 1/4 cup butter (no substitutes), softened
> 1 egg, lightly beaten
> **Dash salt**
> 1 teaspoon vanilla extract
> 1-1/2 cups crisp rice cereal
> 1/2 cup chopped walnuts
> **Red colored sugar**
> **Green candied cherries *or* green confectioners' icing**

In a skillet, combine dates, coconut, sugar, butter, egg and salt. Cook and stir over medium heat until mixture thickens and reaches 160°, about 5 minutes. Remove from the heat; stir in vanilla, cereal and walnuts. Cool for 10 minutes. With slightly moistened fingers, shape tablespoonfuls into strawberry shapes; roll in red sugar. Place on waxed paper-lined baking sheets. Decorate tops with pieces of green candied cherries or pipe leaves on strawberry tops with green icing. **Yield:** about 4 dozen.

White Chocolate Nut Crackles

Joyce Gething, Pampa, Texas

An aunt and I baked a similar cookie often when I was growing up. Through the years, I added the macadamia nuts and white chocolate chips. My family and co-workers rave about these.

> 1/2 cup butter *or* margarine, softened
> 1/2 cup shortening
> 1/2 cup sugar
> 1/2 cup packed brown sugar
> 1 egg
> 1 teaspoon vanilla extract
> 2 cups all-purpose flour
> 1 teaspoon baking soda
> 1 teaspoon cream of tartar
> 1/2 teaspoon salt
> 6 squares (1 ounce *each*) white baking chocolate, coarsely chopped
> 1/2 cup coarsely chopped macadamia nuts, toasted
> **Additional sugar**

In a mixing bowl, cream butter, shortening and sugars. Beat in the egg and vanilla. Combine flour, baking soda, cream of tartar and salt; gradually add to the creamed mixture. Stir in chocolate and nuts. Cover and refrigerate for 1 hour or until easy to handle. Roll into 1-in. balls. Dip each ball halfway in water, then in sugar. Place sugar side up 2 in. apart on ungreased baking sheets; flatten slightly. Bake at 400° for 8-10 minutes or until golden brown. Remove to wire racks to cool. **Yield:** 5-1/2 dozen.

Triple Chocolate Caramel Cookies

Colleen Jennings, Freeburg, Illinois

(Pictured at left)

I love caramel, chocolate and pecans together. While I had recipes for cake, cheesecake and candy that feature this combination, I didn't have one for cookies. So I came up with this recipe.

> 1-1/2 cups butter (no substitutes), softened
> 1 cup sugar
> 1 egg
> 1 teaspoon vanilla extract
> 3 cups all-purpose flour
> 1/2 cup baking cocoa
> 1 package (12 ounces) miniature semisweet chocolate chips
> 1 cup chopped pecans, toasted
> 1 bottle (12-1/2 ounces) caramel ice cream topping
> 4 to 6 ounces dark chocolate confectionary coating,* melted

In a mixing bowl, cream butter and sugar. Beat in egg and vanilla. Combine flour and cocoa; gradually add to the creamed mixture. Stir in chocolate chips and pecans. Roll into 1-in. balls. Place 2 in. apart on ungreased baking sheets. Using the end of a wooden spoon handle, make a 3/8- to 1/2-in.-deep indentation in the center of each ball. Smooth any cracks. Fill each indentation half full with caramel topping. Bake at 350° for 15-18 minutes or until caramel is very bubbly and cookies are set. Cool for 5 minutes before removing to wire racks. Drizzle cooled cookies with confectionary coating. **Yield:** 6 dozen. ***Editor's Note:** Confectionary coating is found in the baking section of most grocery stores. It is sometimes labeled "candy coating" and is often sold in bulk packages of 1 to 1-1/2 pounds.

Butter Pecan Cookies

Martha Thefield, Cedartown, Georgia

(Pictured at left)

When my daughter was a teen, these cookies earned her two blue ribbons from two county fairs. Then a few years ago, her own

> BAKING BONANZA. Pictured at left, clockwise from top: Triple Chocolate Caramel Cookies, Butter Pecan Cookies (recipes on this page) and Chocolate-Dipped Spritz (recipe on page 62).

daughter took home a blue ribbon for the same cookie. Needless to say, these mouth-watering morsels are real winners!

> 1-3/4 cups chopped pecans
> 1 tablespoon plus 1 cup butter (no substitutes), softened, *divided*
> 1 cup packed brown sugar
> 1 egg, *separated*
> 1 teaspoon vanilla extract
> 2 cups self-rising flour*
> 1 cup pecan halves

Place chopped pecans and 1 tablespoon butter in a baking pan. Bake at 325° for 5-7 minutes or until toasted and browned, stirring frequently. Set aside to cool. In a mixing bowl, cream brown sugar and remaining butter. Beat in egg yolk and vanilla. Gradually add flour. Cover and refrigerate for 1 hour or until easy to handle. Roll into 1-in. balls, then roll in toasted pecans, pressing nuts into dough. Place 2 in. apart on ungreased baking sheets. Beat egg white until foamy. Dip pecan halves in egg white, then gently press one into each ball. Bake at 375° for 10-12 minutes or until golden brown. Cool for 2 minutes before removing to wire racks. **Yield:** about 4 dozen. ***Editor's Note:** As a substitute for *each cup* of self-rising flour, place 1-1/2 teaspoons baking powder and 1/2 teaspoon salt in a measuring cup. Add all-purpose flour to measure 1 cup.

Soft Chocolate Cookies

Beth Struble, Bryan, Ohio

My family expects the cookie jar to be filled with home-baked goodies year-round. They don't care for nuts but can't resist chocolate. So these cake-like cookies have become their favorite.

> 1 cup butter *or* margarine, softened
> 1-1/2 cups sugar
> 2 eggs
> 2 teaspoons vanilla extract
> 2 cups all-purpose flour
> 2/3 cup baking cocoa
> 3/4 teaspoon baking soda
> 1/2 teaspoon salt
> Confectioners' sugar

In a mixing bowl, cream butter and sugar. Add eggs, one at a time, beating well after each addition. Beat in vanilla. Combine the flour, cocoa, baking soda and salt; gradually add to creamed mixture. Cover and refrigerate for 1 hour or until easy to handle. Roll into 1-in. balls. Place 2 in. apart on ungreased baking sheets. Flatten with a fork if desired. Bake at 350° for 8-10 minutes or until the edges are firm. Remove to wire racks. Dust warm cookies with confectioners' sugar. **Yield:** 5-1/2 dozen.

Chocolate-Dipped Spritz

Nancy Ross, Alvordton, Ohio

(Pictured on page 60)

Some of my sisters and I get together for a weekend during the holidays to do nothing but bake cookies. These cookies always make an appearance in the goody baskets that we give as gifts.

    1 cup butter (no substitutes), softened
  3/4 cup sugar
    1 egg
    1 teaspoon vanilla extract
2-1/4 cups all-purpose flour
  1/2 teaspoon salt
  1/4 teaspoon baking powder
   11 ounces dark, white *or* milk chocolate
       confectionary coating*
Finely chopped walnuts *or* colored sprinkles, optional

In a mixing bowl, cream butter and sugar. Beat in egg and vanilla. Combine flour, salt and baking powder; gradually add to the creamed mixture. Using a cookie press fitted with the disk of your choice, press dough 2 in. apart onto ungreased baking sheets. Bake at 375° for 7-9 minutes or until set (do not brown). Remove to wire racks to cool. Melt confectionary coating; dip each cookie halfway. If desired, sprinkle walnuts or colored sprinkles over chocolate. Place on waxed paper to harden. **Yield:** about 6 dozen. ***Editor's Note:** Confectionary coating is found in the baking section of most grocery stores. It is sometimes labeled "almond bark" or "candy coating" and is often sold in bulk packages of 1 to 1-1/2 pounds.

Gingered Molasses Cookies

Mrs. Donald Mitchell, Fredericksburg, Texas

A nice blend of spices and grated orange peel makes these a little different than your basic molasses cookies. My son loved these when he was growing up.

  1/2 cup butter *or* margarine, softened
  1/4 cup shortening
1-1/4 cups sugar, *divided*
    1 egg
  1/4 cup molasses
  1/2 teaspoon grated orange peel
    2 cups all-purpose flour
    2 teaspoons baking soda
  1/2 teaspoon salt

  1/2 teaspoon ground ginger
  1/2 teaspoon ground cinnamon
  1/4 teaspoon ground cloves

In a mixing bowl, cream butter, shortening and 1 cup sugar. Beat in egg, molasses and orange peel. Combine the dry ingredients; gradually add to creamed mixture. Roll into 1-1/4-in. balls, then in remaining sugar. Place 2 in. apart on ungreased baking sheets. Bake at 350° for 10-12 minutes or until edges are firm and surface cracks. Remove to wire racks to cool. **Yield:** 5-1/2 dozen.

Apricot Sesame Cookies

Jeanne Allen, Webster, New York

This recipe is a favorite of mine to make for special occasions. The cookies freeze beautifully, so they can conveniently be made ahead of time. Substitute peach, strawberry or raspberry jam if you like.

    1 cup butter (no substitutes), softened
  1/2 cup sugar
    1 teaspoon almond extract
    2 cups all-purpose flour
  1/2 teaspoon salt
    7 tablespoons sesame seeds
    6 tablespoons apricot jam

In a mixing bowl, cream butter and sugar. Beat in extract. Combine the flour and salt; gradually add to the creamed mixture. Roll into 1-in. balls, then roll top and sides in sesame seeds. Place 2 in. apart on ungreased baking sheets. Using the end of a wooden spoon handle, make an indentation in the center of each ball. Fill with jam. Bake at 400° for 10-12 minutes or until lightly browned. Remove to wire racks to cool. **Yield:** 4 dozen.

Fudge-Filled Sandies

Jeanette Ray, Lindenhurst, Illinois

I dream of one day owning a cookie shop. Until then, I'll delight friends and family with my homemade concoctions. These cookies are like pecan sandies, but I've added a touch of delicious chocolate.

    1 cup butter (no substitutes), softened
  3/4 cup confectioners' sugar
    1 teaspoon vanilla extract
    2 cups all-purpose flour
    1 cup finely chopped pecans
Additional confectioners' sugar
FILLING:
  3/4 cup semisweet chocolate chips

2 tablespoons light corn syrup
1 tablespoon water
1 tablespoon shortening

In a mixing bowl, cream butter and sugar. Beat in vanilla. Combine flour and pecans; gradually add to the creamed mixture. Roll into 1-in. balls. Place 1 in. apart on ungreased baking sheets. Using the end of a wooden spoon handle, make an indentation in the center of each. Bake at 325° for 18-20 minutes or until lightly browned. Roll warm cookies in confectioners' sugar; cool on wire racks. In a microwave or double boiler, melt chocolate chips; stir in remaining filling ingredients until smooth. Spoon into cooled cookies. **Yield:** 4 dozen.

Chocolate Chip Almond Cookies

Mary Schneeberg, Oconomowoc, Wisconsin

My husband likes the flavor and texture of these cookies. Milk chocolate chips and sliced almonds make them deliciously different. My mother-in-law shared the recipe with me.

1/2 cup butter *or* margarine, softened
1/2 cup packed dark brown sugar
1/3 cup sugar
1 egg
1 teaspoon vanilla extract
1 cup plus 2 tablespoons all-purpose flour
1/2 teaspoon salt
1/4 teaspoon baking soda
1 cup milk chocolate chips
1 cup sliced almonds

In a mixing bowl, cream butter and sugars. Beat in egg and vanilla. Combine flour, salt and baking soda; gradually add to the creamed mixture. Stir in chocolate chips and almonds. Roll into 1-in. balls. Place 2 in. apart on greased baking sheets. Bake at 375° for 9-11 minutes or until edges are firm. Remove to wire racks to cool. **Yield:** 4 dozen.

Scandinavian Drops

Naomi Falcone, Lancaster, Pennsylvania

This traditional recipe has been in the family for years. Every Christmas, friends and family expect to see these attractive and delicious cookies on the table. I always happily oblige!

1 cup butter (no substitutes), softened
1/2 cup packed brown sugar

2 eggs, *separated*
1 teaspoon vanilla extract
2-1/3 cups all-purpose flour
1 cup finely chopped walnuts
1/2 to 2/3 cup jam *or* jelly of your choice

In a mixing bowl, cream butter and brown sugar. Add egg yolks, one at a time, beating well after each addition. Beat in vanilla. Gradually add flour. Roll into 1-in. balls. Beat egg whites until foamy. Dip each ball halfway into egg whites, then into walnuts. Place nut side up 2 in. apart on ungreased baking sheets. Using the end of a wooden spoon handle, make an indentation in the center of each. Bake at 375° for 10-12 minutes or until lightly browned. Remove to wire racks. Fill with jam; cool. **Yield:** 5-1/2 dozen.

Chocolate Puddles

Kathie Griffin, Antelope, California

The variations on this original recipe are almost endless. For double chocolate puddles, use semisweet chocolate chips for the vanilla chips. Or make peanut butter puddles by substituting peanut butter chips and peanuts for the vanilla chips and mixed nuts.

1 cup butter (no substitutes), softened
1 cup sugar
1 cup packed brown sugar
2 eggs
2 teaspoons vanilla extract
3 cups all-purpose flour
3/4 cup baking cocoa
1 teaspoon baking soda
FILLING:
1 cup vanilla chips
1/2 cup plus 2 tablespoons sweetened condensed milk
3/4 cup coarsely chopped mixed nuts

In a mixing bowl, cream butter and sugars. Add the eggs, one at a time, beating well after each addition. Beat in vanilla. Combine flour, cocoa and baking soda; gradually add to the creamed mixture. Cover and refrigerate for 2 hours or until dough is stiff. Meanwhile, for filling, heat chips and milk in a heavy saucepan over low heat until chips are melted, stirring constantly. Stir in nuts. Cover and refrigerate for 1 hour or until easy to handle. Roll cookie dough into 1-1/4-in. balls. Place 2 in. apart on lightly greased baking sheets. Using the end of a wooden spoon handle, make an indentation in the center; smooth any cracks. Roll filling into 1/2-in. balls; gently push one into each cookie. Bake at 375° for 8-10 minutes or until cookies are set. Remove to wire racks to cool. **Yield:** about 5 dozen.

Cinnamon Chip Cookies

Barbara Ehlers, Florence, Wisconsin

I've had this recipe for more than 40 years but can't recall its origin. Cinnamon, chocolate chips and orange peel pair nicely in these outstanding cookies.

    1 cup butter *or* margarine, softened
    1 cup sugar
    1 egg yolk
    1 teaspoon grated orange peel
    1 teaspoon vanilla extract
    2 cups all-purpose flour
    1 tablespoon ground cinnamon
    1 teaspoon baking powder
    1/4 teaspoon salt
    1 cup (6 ounces) semisweet chocolate chips
    1/2 cup chopped nuts
    2 egg whites, beaten
Additional sugar

In a mixing bowl, cream butter and sugar. Beat in egg yolk, orange peel and vanilla. Combine the flour, cinnamon, baking powder and salt; gradually add to the creamed mixture. Stir in chocolate chips and nuts (dough will be very stiff). Roll into 1-1/2-in. balls. Roll in egg whites, then in sugar. Place 2 in. apart on greased and floured baking sheets. Bake at 350° for 12-14 minutes or until lightly browned. Remove to wire racks to cool. **Yield:** 5-1/2 dozen.

Almond Cherry Biscotti

Beatrice Reid, Scottsbluff, Nebraska

I love baking all kinds of cookies, but since I'm Italian, biscotti is my all-time favorite. I remember nibbling on these as a child each Christmas.

    2 cups all-purpose flour
    1 cup sugar
    1/2 teaspoon baking powder
    1/2 teaspoon salt
    1/4 cup cold butter (no substitutes)
    2 eggs
    1 tablespoon milk
    1/2 teaspoon vanilla extract
    1 cup coarsely chopped blanched almonds
    1 cup halved candied cherries

In a bowl, combine the flour, sugar, baking powder and salt. Cut in butter until mixture resembles coarse crumbs. In another bowl, beat eggs, milk and vanilla until blended; stir into dry ingredients until blended. Stir in almonds and cherries (the dough will be crumbly). Divide dough in half; shape each half into a ball. On an ungreased baking sheet, roll each ball into a 10-in. x 2-1/2-in. rectangle. Bake at 350° for 30-35 minutes or until golden brown. Carefully remove to wire racks; cool for 20 minutes. Transfer to a cutting board; cut diagonally with a sharp knife into 3/4-in. slices. Place cut side down on ungreased baking sheets. Bake for 15 minutes or until firm. Remove to wire racks to cool. Store in an airtight container. **Yield:** 2 dozen.

Crisp 'n' Chewy Cookies

Kristen Snyder, Sugar Land, Texas

Knowing I'm a cookie lover, my mother-in-law sent me this recipe years ago. Many folks have told me these are the best cookies they've ever tasted. I think it's the Butterfinger candy bars that make them so special.

1-1/4 cups butter-flavored shortening
    3/4 cup sugar
    3/4 cup packed brown sugar
    1 egg
    3 tablespoons maple syrup
    1 teaspoon vanilla extract
    3 cups quick-cooking oats
1-3/4 cups all-purpose flour
    1 teaspoon baking soda
    1 teaspoon salt
    3/4 cup semisweet chocolate chips
    2 Butterfinger candy bars (2.1 ounces *each*), chopped

In a mixing bowl, cream shortening and sugars. Beat in egg, syrup and vanilla. Combine oats, flour, baking soda and salt; gradually add to the creamed mixture. Stir in chocolate chips and candy bars. Roll into 1-in. balls. Place 2 in. apart on ungreased baking sheets. Bake at 375° for 7-9 minutes or until golden brown. Remove to wire racks to cool. **Yield:** 7 dozen.

Big Soft Ginger Cookies

Barbara Heinze, Boise, Idaho

These nicely spiced soft cookies are perfect for folks who like the flavor of ginger but don't care for crunchy gingersnaps.

    3/4 cup butter (no substitutes), softened
    1 cup sugar
    1 egg
    1/4 cup molasses
2-1/4 cups all-purpose flour

2 teaspoons ground ginger
1 teaspoon baking soda
3/4 teaspoon ground cinnamon
1/2 teaspoon ground cloves
1/4 teaspoon salt
Additional sugar

In a mixing bowl, cream butter and sugar. Beat in egg and molasses. Combine the flour, ginger, baking soda, cinnamon, cloves and salt; gradually add to the creamed mixture. Roll into 1-1/2-in. balls, then roll in sugar. Place 2 in. apart on ungreased baking sheets. Bake at 350° for 10-12 minutes or until puffy and lightly browned. Remove to wire racks to cool. **Yield:** 2-1/2 dozen.

No-Bake Apricot Snowballs

Barbara Sessoyeff, Redwood Valley, California

Since it's just the two of us at home, I share these sweet snowballs with friends and neighbors, who gladly accept them. I appreciate the no-bake convenience.

   2 cups flaked coconut
1-1/2 cups dried apricots
   1 cup golden raisins
  1/3 cup orange juice
   3 tablespoons grated orange peel
1-1/2 cups coarsely chopped blanched almonds, toasted
Confectioners' sugar

In a food processor or blender, combine the first five ingredients. Cover and process until mixture is finely chopped and well blended. Stir in almonds. Roll into 1-in. balls, then roll in confectioners' sugar. Let dry on wire racks for about 1 hour. Store in an airtight container. **Yield:** 5-1/2 dozen.

Cloverleaf Cookies

Patricia Gilbert, Kansas City, Missouri

This recipe is a favorite of kids because they get three cookies in one! Combining three different flavors of dough—chocolate chip, peanut butter and chocolate —is a fun and tasty idea.

1/2 cup butter *or* margarine, softened
1/2 cup shortening
3/4 cup packed brown sugar
1/2 cup sugar
   1 egg
1-1/2 teaspoons vanilla extract
1-3/4 cups all-purpose flour

1 teaspoon baking soda
1/2 teaspoon salt
1/2 cup miniature semisweet chocolate chips
1/4 cup chunky peanut butter
   1 square (1 ounce) unsweetened chocolate, melted and cooled

In a mixing bowl, cream butter, shortening and sugars. Beat in egg and vanilla. Combine flour, baking soda and salt; gradually add to the creamed mixture. Divide dough into thirds. Add chocolate chips to one portion, peanut butter to another and melted chocolate to the third portion. Cover and refrigerate for 2 hours or until firm. Roll 1/2 teaspoonfuls of dough into balls. For each cookie, place three balls (one of each dough) with edges touching on ungreased baking sheets to form a cloverleaf. Place cookies 2 in. apart. Bake at 375° for 10-12 minutes or until golden brown. Cool for 1 minute before removing to wire racks. **Yield:** 5 dozen.

Mocha-Pecan Butter Balls

Kathleen Pruitt, Hoopeston, Illinois

When I was a little girl, one of my mother's co-workers would bring tins of assorted Christmas cookies for my sister and me. These were the ones I reached for first.

2/3 cup butter (no substitutes), softened
   1 package (3 ounces) cream cheese, softened
2/3 cup instant chocolate drink mix
1/3 cup confectioners' sugar
   1 teaspoon instant coffee granules
   2 teaspoons vanilla extract
1-3/4 cups all-purpose flour
  1/4 teaspoon salt
   1 cup finely chopped pecans
Additional confectioners' sugar

In a mixing bowl, cream butter, cream cheese, drink mix, sugar and coffee granules. Beat in vanilla. Combine flour and salt; gradually add to creamed mixture. Stir in pecans. Cover and refrigerate for 1 hour or until easy to handle. Roll into 1-in. balls. Place 1 in. apart on ungreased baking sheets. Bake at 350° for 15-18 minutes or until firm. Cool on pan for 1-2 minutes. Roll warm cookies in confectioners' sugar; cool on wire racks. **Yield:** 4 dozen.

IF YOUR PRESSED COOKIE DOUGH is too soft and not making a sharp design, refrigerate the dough briefly. If the dough is too stiff and won't move through the press, let the dough stand at room temperature until it is the right consistency.

Cocoa Surprise Cookies

Debra Himes, Cedar Rapids, Iowa

These rich cookies are truly a chocolate lover's delight. Miniature marshmallows are the delectable surprise in every bite.

- **1 cup butter (no substitutes), softened**
- **1 cup sugar**
- **1 cup packed brown sugar**
- **2 eggs**
- **2 teaspoons vanilla extract**
- **3 cups all-purpose flour**
- **2/3 cup baking cocoa**
- **1/2 teaspoon baking soda**
- **2 cups (12 ounces) semisweet chocolate chips**
- **2 cups miniature marshmallows, frozen**

In a mixing bowl, cream butter and sugars. Add the eggs, one at a time, beating well after each addition. Beat in vanilla. Combine flour, cocoa and baking soda; gradually add to the creamed mixture. Stir in chocolate chips. Roll into 1-1/2-in. balls. Press two to three frozen marshmallows into each; reshape balls. Place 2 in. apart on ungreased baking sheets. Bake at 400° for 8-10 minutes or until set. Cool for 5 minutes before removing to wire racks. **Yield:** 5 dozen.

Peppermint Snowballs

Susan Bonnstetter, Slayton, Minnesota

The holidays don't begin around our house until a batch of these cookies is baking in the oven. Their wonderful aroma scrumptiously says, "Christmas!"

- **1 cup butter (no substitutes), softened**
- **1/2 cup confectioners' sugar**
- **1 teaspoon vanilla extract**
- **2-1/2 cups all-purpose flour**
- **1/2 cup ground nuts, optional**

FILLING:
- **2 tablespoons cream cheese, softened**
- **1/2 cup confectioners' sugar**
- **1 teaspoon milk**
- **3 tablespoons crushed peppermint candy**
- **1 drop red food coloring, optional**

TOPPING:
- **1/2 cup crushed peppermint candy**
- **1/2 cup confectioners' sugar**

In a mixing bowl, cream butter and sugar. Beat in vanilla. Gradually add flour. Stir in nuts if desired. Knead dough until pliable. Cover and refrigerate for

1 hour or until easy to handle. In a mixing bowl, beat cream cheese, sugar, milk, candy and food coloring if desired. Roll tablespoonfuls of dough into balls. Using the end of a wooden spoon handle, make a deep indentation in the center of each. Fill with 1/4 teaspoon filling. Cover with 1/4 teaspoonfuls of dough; seal and reshape into balls. Combine topping ingredients; roll balls in topping. Place 1 in. apart on ungreased baking sheets. Bake at 350° for 12-14 minutes or until firm. Roll warm cookies in topping again; cool on wire racks. **Yield:** 4 dozen.

Cinnamon Almond Crescents

Jennifer Branum, O'Fallon, Illinois

I set out these cookies as we open our gifts on Christmas Eve. Before long, the plate is empty and I'm being asked to refill it!

- **1 cup butter (no substitutes), softened**
- **1/3 cup sugar**
- **1/2 teaspoon vanilla extract**
- **1-2/3 cups all-purpose flour**
- **1/2 cup finely ground blanched almonds**

TOPPING:
- **1/2 cup sugar**
- **1/2 teaspoon ground cinnamon**

In a mixing bowl, cream butter and sugar. Beat in vanilla. Combine flour and almonds; gradually add to creamed mixture. Roll into 1-in. balls; shape into crescents. Place 2 in. apart on lightly greased baking sheets. Bake at 350° for 10-12 minutes or until set (do not brown). Combine sugar and cinnamon in a small bowl. Roll warm cookies in cinnamon-sugar; cool on wire racks. **Yield:** about 3-1/2 dozen.

Dad's Oatmeal Cookies

Jean Newell, Lakewood, Washington

Among Mother's old newspaper clippings and recipes scribbled on the back of envelopes, I came across this treasured recipe. It always gives me a warm feeling when I go through her recipe box, and I have fond memories of her baking these cookies.

- **1 cup butter (no substitutes), softened**
- **1 cup sugar**
- **1/2 cup packed brown sugar**
- **1 egg**
- **1 teaspoon vanilla extract**

Shaped Specialties

1-1/2 cups all-purpose flour
1-1/4 cups quick-cooking oats
  1 cup Grape Nuts cereal
  1 teaspoon baking soda
  1 teaspoon baking powder

In a mixing bowl, cream butter and sugars. Beat in egg and vanilla. Combine flour, oats, cereal, baking soda and baking powder; gradually add to creamed mixture. Roll into 3/4-in. balls. Place 2 in. apart on ungreased baking sheets; flatten with a fork. Bake at 375° for 10-12 minutes or until lightly browned. Cool for 3 minutes before removing to wire racks. **Yield:** about 6 dozen.

Christmas Casserole Cookies

Vera Link, Reeds Spring, Missouri

The batter for these specialty cookies is baked and then formed into balls. When my son-in-law and grandson are coming for a visit, I'm always sure to have these cookies on hand.

  3 eggs
  1 cup sugar
  1 teaspoon vanilla extract
1/4 teaspoon almond extract
  1 cup chopped dates
  1 cup flaked coconut
  1 cup chopped walnuts
Additional sugar

In a mixing bowl, beat eggs until lemon-colored. Gradually beat in sugar. Beat in extracts. Stir in the dates, coconut and walnuts. Pour into an ungreased deep 2-qt. baking dish. Bake at 350° for 30-35 minutes. Remove from oven; stir with a wooden spoon (batter will appear moist and sticky). Place baking dish on a wire rack. When cool enough to handle, roll batter into 1-in. balls. Roll in sugar; place on waxed paper-lined baking sheets. **Yield:** 4 dozen.

Nutty Orange Spritz Strips

Jeannie Mayfield, Santa Rosa, California

While living in Wisconsin years ago, I participated in an annual cookie exchange with my co-workers, and the other women raved about these. The unique recipe now holds a treasured place in our family cookbook.

3/4 cup butter (no substitutes), softened
  1 cup sugar
  1 egg

  4 teaspoons grated orange peel
2-3/4 cups all-purpose flour
  1 teaspoon baking powder
1/4 teaspoon salt
  2 tablespoons orange juice
  1 cup (6 ounces) semisweet chocolate chips
  1 tablespoon shortening
  1 cup ground walnuts

In a mixing bowl, cream butter and sugar. Beat in egg and orange peel. Combine flour, baking powder and salt; add to the creamed mixture alternately with orange juice. Using a cookie press fitted with a bar disk, form dough into long strips on ungreased baking sheets. Cut each strip into 3-in. pieces (there is no need to separate the pieces). Bake at 350° for 12-14 minutes or until edges are golden. Cut into pieces again if necessary. Remove to wire racks to cool. Melt chocolate and shortening in a microwave or double boiler; stir until smooth. Dip each end of cookies in chocolate mixture, then in walnuts. Place on waxed paper; let stand until hardened. **Yield:** about 4-1/2 dozen.

Fudgy Chocolate Balls

Amy Stevenson, Elkton, Maryland

These cookies may be small, but every bite is packed with big chocolate flavor. I sometimes dip the tops of the cookies in the frosting instead of spreading the frosting on top.

1/3 cup butter (no substitutes)
  2 squares (1 ounce *each*) unsweetened chocolate
  1 cup sugar
  1 egg plus 1 egg yolk, beaten
1/2 teaspoon vanilla extract
1-1/3 cups all-purpose flour
1/2 cup chopped walnuts
FROSTING:
  1 square (1 ounce) unsweetened chocolate
  1 tablespoon butter (no substitutes)
  1 cup confectioners' sugar
1/4 teaspoon vanilla
  2 to 3 tablespoons milk

In a large microwave-safe bowl, melt butter and chocolate. Stir in sugar, egg, egg yolk and vanilla; mix well. Gradually add flour. Stir in walnuts. Roll into 3/4-in. balls. Place 2 in. apart on ungreased baking sheets. Bake at 350° for 8-10 minutes or until firm. Remove to wire racks. For frosting, melt chocolate and butter in a microwave-safe bowl. Stir in sugar, vanilla and enough milk to achieve spreading consistency. Frost cooled cookies. **Yield:** 5 dozen.

Snow-Topped Chocolate Mint Cookies

Arlene Hurst, Ephrata, Pennsylvania

(Pictured at left)

Our local newspaper had a cookie contest a while back. This was one of the recipes featured, and it caught my eye because I love mint flavor. My family likes these cookies as much as I do.

> 1 package (10 ounces) mint semisweet chocolate chips, *divided*
> 6 tablespoons butter (no substitutes), softened
> 1 cup sugar
> 2 eggs
> 1-1/2 teaspoons vanilla extract
> 1-1/2 cups all-purpose flour
> 1-1/2 teaspoons baking powder
> 1/4 teaspoon salt
> Confectioners' sugar

In a microwave, melt 1 cup chocolate chips; set aside to cool. In a mixing bowl, cream butter and sugar. Add eggs, one at a time, beating well after each addition. Beat in the melted chocolate chips and vanilla. Combine flour, baking powder and salt; gradually add to the creamed mixture. Stir in the remaining chocolate chips. Cover and refrigerate for 2 hours or until easy to handle. Roll into 1-in. balls, then roll in confectioners' sugar. Place 2 in. apart on ungreased baking sheets. Bake at 350° for 10-12 minutes or until edges are set and centers are almost set. Cool for 10 minutes before removing to wire racks. **Yield:** 4 dozen.

Sugar Gems

Mary Lou Ballentine, Madison, Wisconsin

(Pictured at left)

If you don't have much luck with rolled sugar cookies, give these a try. Oil and confectioners' sugar give them a unique crispness.

> 1 cup shortening
> 1 cup vegetable oil
> 1 cup sugar
> 1 cup confectioners' sugar
> 2 eggs

YULETIDE TREATS. Pictured at left, top to bottom: Snow-Topped Chocolate Mint Cookies (recipe on this page), Jeweled Thumbprints (recipe on page 70), Sugar Gems and Cherry Snowballs (both recipes on this page).

> 1 teaspoon vanilla extract
> 4-1/2 cups all-purpose flour
> 1 teaspoon baking soda
> 1 teaspoon cream of tartar
> 1/2 teaspoon salt
> Additional sugar *or* colored sugar

In a mixing bowl, cream shortening, oil and sugars. Add eggs, one at a time, beating well after each addition. Beat in vanilla. Combine the flour, baking soda, cream of tartar and salt; gradually add to the creamed mixture. Cover and refrigerate for 1 hour or until easy to handle. Roll into 1-in. balls; dip tops in sugar or colored sugar. Place sugar side up 2 in. apart on ungreased baking sheets. Bake at 350° for 12-14 minutes or until edges begin to brown. Remove to wire racks to cool. **Yield:** about 7 dozen.

FOR BEST RESULTS, use shortening, butter only or margarine (containing at least 80% oil) as directed for the cookie. Whipped, tub, soft, liquid or reduced-fat products contain air and water and will produce flat, tough or underbrowned cookies.

Cherry Snowballs

Evy Adams, West Seneca, New York

(Pictured at left)

A juicy maraschino cherry is the pleasant surprise tucked inside these unique cookies. My mother clipped this recipe out of the newspaper more than 30 years ago.

> 1 cup butter (no substitutes), softened
> 1/2 cup confectioners' sugar
> 1 tablespoon water
> 1 teaspoon vanilla extract
> 2 cups all-purpose flour
> 1 cup quick-cooking oats
> 1/2 teaspoon salt
> 36 maraschino cherries, well drained
> **COATING:**
> 2 cups confectioners' sugar
> 1/4 to 1/3 cup milk
> 2 cups flaked coconut, finely chopped

In a mixing bowl, cream butter, sugar, water and vanilla. Combine flour, oats and salt; gradually add to the creamed mixture. Shape a tablespoonful of dough around each cherry, forming a ball. Place 2 in. apart on ungreased baking sheets. Bake at 350° for 18-20 minutes or until bottoms are browned. Remove to wire racks to cool. Combine sugar and enough milk to achieve smooth dipping consistency. Dip cookies, then roll in coconut. **Yield:** 3 dozen.

Jeweled Thumbprints

Maria Debono, New York, New York

(Pictured on page 68)

When I moved here from Malta more than 20 years ago, a kind neighbor lady took me under her wing and baked many cookies for me. This is one of her recipes that I treasure.

    3/4 cup butter (no substitutes), softened
    3/4 cup confectioners' sugar
      1 egg yolk
    1/2 teaspoon almond extract
1-3/4 cups all-purpose flour
    1/2 cup raspberry *or* apricot preserves

In a mixing bowl, cream butter and sugar. Beat in egg yolk and extract. Gradually add flour. Cover and refrigerate for 2 hours or until easy to handle. Roll into 3/4-in. balls. Place 1 in. apart on greased baking sheets. Using the end of a wooden spoon handle, make an indentation in the center of each ball. Bake at 350° for 12-14 minutes or until edges are lightly browned. Remove to wire racks to cool. Fill with preserves. **Yield:** 6 dozen.

Oatmeal Fruit Cookies

Brenda Cline, Cody, Wyoming

I've been using this recipe for more than 25 years, so I don't have to tell you how much my family likes it! Whole wheat flour and oats make these crisp yet chewy cookies a hearty around-the-clock snack.

      1 cup butter *or* margarine, softened
      1 cup sugar
      1 cup packed brown sugar
      2 eggs
      1 teaspoon vanilla extract
      4 cups old-fashioned oats
      1 cup whole wheat flour
      1 teaspoon baking soda
    1/2 teaspoon salt
    1/2 teaspoon ground cinnamon
      1 cup raisins
      1 cup chopped walnuts
      1 cup flaked coconut
      1 cup chopped dates

In a mixing bowl, cream butter and sugars. Add eggs, one at a time, beating well after each addition. Beat in vanilla. Combine oats, flour, baking soda, salt and cinnamon; gradually add to the creamed mixture. Stir in raisins, walnuts, coconut and dates.

Roll into 1-1/2-in. balls. Place 2 in. apart on ungreased baking sheets. Bake at 325° for 14-16 minutes or until edges are firm. Remove to wire racks to cool. **Yield:** about 3-1/2 dozen.

Almond Butter Cookies

Lynne Romyn, Fayetteville, North Carolina

I came up with this cookie recipe as a way to capture a butter cake popular in my husband's native Netherlands. Almond paste and butter make each melt-in-your-mouth morsel irresistible.

    1/2 cup butter (no substitutes), softened
    1/2 cup shortening
      6 ounces almond paste
1-1/3 cups sugar
      1 egg
      2 cups all-purpose flour
      1 teaspoon baking soda

In a mixing bowl, cream butter, shortening, almond paste and sugar. Beat in egg. Combine flour and baking soda; gradually add to the creamed mixture. Roll into 1/4-in. balls. Place 2 in. apart on ungreased baking sheets. Bake at 400° for 8-10 minutes or until lightly browned. Remove to wire racks to cool. **Yield:** 6-1/2 dozen.

Shamrock Cookies

Mardell Magorian, Patterson, California

My kids have fun helping me make these cute cookies. Although these festive morsels are really meant for St. Patrick's Day, my family requests them year-round.

    3/4 cup butter (no substitutes), softened
    2/3 cup sugar
      1 egg
    1/4 teaspoon peppermint extract
Green food coloring
      2 cups all-purpose flour
    1/4 teaspoon salt
Green colored sugar

In a mixing bowl, cream butter and sugar. Beat in egg, extract and food coloring. Combine flour and salt; gradually add to the creamed mixture. Shape into three 8-in. logs; roll in colored sugar. Wrap each in plastic wrap; refrigerate for 2 hours or until firm. Unwrap and cut into 1/4-in. slices. To form shamrocks, place three slices with sides touching 1 in. apart on ungreased baking sheets. Use a portion of another slice for stem. Bake at 350° for 12-14 minutes or until edges are lightly browned. Remove to wire racks to cool. **Yield:** 2-1/2 dozen.

Double Nut Crunchies

Pia Harrison, Green Valley, Arizona

Chopped cashews lend to the delectable crunch of these cookies, while peanut butter gives them even more great nutty flavor.

> 1 cup butter-flavored shortening
> 1 cup chunky peanut butter
> 1 cup sugar
> 1 cup packed brown sugar
> 2 eggs
> 1 teaspoon vanilla extract
> 2 cups all-purpose flour
> 1/2 cup baking cocoa
> 2 teaspoons baking soda
> Pinch salt
> 1 cup coarsely chopped salted cashews

In a mixing bowl, cream shortening, peanut butter and sugars. Add the eggs, one at a time, beating well after each addition. Beat in vanilla. Combine flour, cocoa, baking soda and salt; gradually add to the creamed mixture. Stir in cashews. Roll into 1-in. balls. Place 2 in. apart on ungreased baking sheets. Flatten with a fork dipped in sugar. Bake at 350° for 8-10 minutes or until lightly browned. Remove to wire racks to cool. **Yield:** about 5 dozen.

Chocolate Pecan Dreams

Becky Ratzlaff, Newton, Kansas

This recipe began as the base for a peanut butter chocolate thumbprint. I liked it so much, though, I decided to turn it into its own cookie recipe.

> 1-1/3 cups shortening
> 1 cup sugar
> 2 eggs, *separated*
> 2 tablespoons milk
> 1 teaspoon vanilla extract
> 2 cups all-purpose flour
> 1/2 cup baking cocoa
> 3/4 teaspoon salt
> 2/3 cup miniature semisweet chocolate chips
> 1-1/4 cups coarsely chopped pecans

In a mixing bowl, cream shortening and sugar. Beat in egg yolks, milk and vanilla. Combine flour, cocoa and salt; gradually add to the creamed mixture. Stir in chocolate chips. Roll into 1-1/2-in. balls. Beat egg whites until foamy. Dip each ball halfway into egg

whites, then in pecans. Place pecan side up 2 in. apart on greased baking sheets. Flatten slightly with a glass dipped in sugar. Bake at 350° for 12-14 minutes or until firm. Carefully remove to wire racks to cool. **Yield:** 5 dozen.

Buttery Yeast Spritz

Janet Stucky, Sterling, Illinois

Yeast may be an unusual ingredient for cookies, but the buttery flavor is fabulous. These were my mother's favorite cookies…now I make them for my children and grandchildren.

> 1 package (1/4 ounce) active dry yeast
> 2 tablespoons warm water (110° to 115°)
> 2 cups butter (no substitutes), softened
> 1 cup sugar
> 2 egg yolks
> 4 cups all-purpose flour

In a bowl, dissolve yeast in water; set aside. In a mixing bowl, cream butter and sugar. Beat in egg yolks and yeast mixture. Gradually add flour. Using a cookie press fitted with disk of your choice, press dough into desired shapes 1 in. apart onto ungreased baking sheets. Bake at 400° for 7-9 minutes or until lightly browned. Remove to wire racks to cool. **Yield:** 13 dozen.

Crispy Orange-Almond Cookies

Lynn Olson, Eau Claire, Wisconsin

I like to serve these light crispy cookies with ice cream or sherbet. The recipe is a personal favorite because it came from a good friend.

> 1 cup shortening
> 1/2 cup sugar
> 1/2 cup packed brown sugar
> 1 egg
> 2 tablespoons orange juice
> 1 tablespoon grated orange peel
> 1/2 teaspoon almond extract
> 2-1/3 cups all-purpose flour
> 1/2 teaspoon baking soda
> 1/4 cup chopped almonds

In a mixing bowl, cream shortening and sugars. Beat in egg, orange juice, peel and extract. Combine flour and baking soda; gradually add to the creamed mixture. Stir in almonds. Roll into 1-in. balls. Place 2 in. apart on ungreased baking sheets. Bake at 375° for 8-10 minutes or until lightly browned. Remove to wire racks to cool. **Yield:** 6-1/2 dozen.

Cinnamon Almond Strips

Fred Grover, Lake Havasu City, Arizona

When I was young, I could hardly wait for the holidays because I knew these rich cookies would make an appearance on the cookie tray. Now I make them for holidays throughout the year.

1-1/2 cups butter (no substitutes), softened
  1 cup sugar
  3 eggs, *separated*
  3 cups all-purpose flour
TOPPING:
1-1/2 cups sugar
  1 cup finely chopped almonds
1-1/2 teaspoons ground cinnamon

In a mixing bowl, cream butter and sugar. Beat in egg yolks; mix well. Gradually add flour. Using a cookie press fitted with a bar disk, press dough into long strips onto ungreased baking sheets. Beat egg whites until stiff; brush over dough. Combine topping ingredients; sprinkle over strips. Cut each strip into 2-in. pieces (there is no need to separate the pieces). Bake at 350° for 8-10 minutes or until edges are firm (do not brown). Cut into pieces again if necessary. Remove to wire racks to cool. **Yield:** about 10 dozen.

White Chocolate-Cranberry Biscotti

Brenda Keith, Talent, Oregon

The original version of this recipe was handed down from my great-aunt. Through the years, my mother and I have tried different flavor combinations...this is a favorite for all.

  1/2 cup butter (no substitutes), softened
  1 cup sugar
  4 eggs
  1 teaspoon vanilla extract
  3 cups all-purpose flour
  1 tablespoon baking powder
  3/4 cup dried cranberries
  3/4 cup vanilla chips

In a mixing bowl, cream butter and sugar. Add eggs, one at a time, beating well after each addition. Beat in vanilla. Combine flour and baking powder; gradually add to creamed mixture. Stir in cranberries and vanilla chips. Divide dough into three portions. On ungreased baking sheets, shape each portion into a 10-in. x 2-in. rectangle. Bake at 350° for 20-25 minutes or until lightly browned. Cool for 5 minutes. Transfer to a cutting board; cut diagonally with a serrated knife into 1-in. slices. Place cut side down on ungreased

baking sheets. Bake for 15-20 minutes or until golden brown. Remove to wire racks to cool. Store in an airtight container. **Yield:** 2-1/2 dozen.

Butterscotch Snickerdoodles

Nancy Radenbaugh, White Lake, Michigan

This recipe is a combination of the traditional Snickerdoodle recipe and my mother's best spritz recipe. Everyone comments on the unique combination of ingredients.

  1 cup butter *or* margarine, softened
  1/3 cup vegetable oil
1-1/4 cups sugar
  1/3 cup confectioners' sugar
  2 eggs
  3 tablespoons plain yogurt
1-1/2 teaspoons almond extract
  1/8 teaspoon lemon extract
3-1/2 cups all-purpose flour
  1 cup whole wheat flour
  1 teaspoon cream of tartar
  1 teaspoon baking soda
  1/2 teaspoon salt
  1 cup butterscotch chips
  1/2 cup chopped almonds
Additional sugar

In a mixing bowl, cream butter, oil and sugars. Add eggs, one at a time, beating well after each addition. Add yogurt and extracts. Combine flours, cream of tartar, baking soda and salt; gradually add to the creamed mixture. Stir in butterscotch chips and almonds. Roll into 1-in. balls, then in sugar. Place 2 in. apart on ungreased baking sheets. Flatten with a fork dipped in sugar. Bake at 350° for 12-15 minutes or until lightly browned. Remove to wire racks to cool. **Yield:** 8 dozen.

Chocolate Jubilees

LaVera Fenton, Colorado Springs, Colorado

Rich and fudgy, these cookies make many appearances in care packages I send out. I combined several recipes and added maraschino cherries to come up with this winning recipe.

  1 cup butter *or* margarine, softened
  1 cup shortening
  2 cups packed brown sugar
  1 cup sugar
  4 eggs
  2 to 3 teaspoons almond extract
  4 cups all-purpose flour

1 cup quick-cooking oats
1 cup baking cocoa
2 teaspoons baking soda
2 teaspoons salt
1 jar (16 ounces) maraschino cherries, drained
 and chopped
3 cups (18 ounces) semisweet chocolate chips
1 cup sliced almonds, optional

In a mixing bowl, cream butter, shortening and sugars. Add eggs, one at a time, beating well after each addition. Beat in extract. Combine flour, oats, cocoa, baking soda and salt; gradually add to the creamed mixture. Transfer to a larger bowl if necessary. Stir in cherries, chocolate chips and almonds if desired. Roll into 1-1/2-in. balls. Place 3 in. apart on ungreased baking sheets. Bake at 375° for 12-14 minutes or until the edges are firm. Remove to wire racks to cool. **Yield:** about 5-1/2 dozen.

Pistachio Orange Drops

Susan Zarzycki, Saratoga, California

These shaped sugar cookies are topped with melted chocolate and chopped pistachios, making them a pretty treat for special occasions.

1 cup butter (no substitutes), softened
1 cup confectioners' sugar
1 teaspoon grated orange peel
2 cups all-purpose flour
1 cup finely chopped pistachios
1 cup (6 ounces) semisweet chocolate chips
2 tablespoons shortening

In a mixing bowl, cream butter, sugar and orange peel. Gradually add flour. Set aside 3 tablespoons pistachios for topping; stir remaining pistachios into dough. Roll into 1-in. balls. Place 1-1/2 in. apart on ungreased baking sheets. Bake at 375° for 8-10 minutes or until lightly browned. Remove to wire racks. In a saucepan over low heat, melt chocolate chips and shortening; stir until smooth. Dip tops of cooled cookies in chocolate, then in reserved pistachios. **Yield:** about 4-1/2 dozen.

Chocolate-Filled Crinkles

Deborah Knight, Monroe, Georgia

I had this recipe in my files some time before I finally got around to trying it. I'm glad I did…my family thinks these are the best!

1/2 cup butter (no substitutes), softened
1 cup sugar
1 egg

1-1/2 teaspoons vanilla extract
1-1/2 cups all-purpose flour
1/2 cup baking cocoa
1/4 teaspoon salt
1/4 teaspoon baking powder
1/4 teaspoon baking soda
FILLING:
1 cup (6 ounces) semisweet chocolate chips
1/2 cup sweetened condensed milk
1/4 cup finely chopped pecans
1/4 cup flaked coconut
2 to 3 teaspoons milk

In a mixing bowl, cream butter and sugar. Beat in egg and vanilla. Combine flour, cocoa, salt, baking powder and baking soda; gradually add to the creamed mixture. Roll into 1-in. balls. Place 2 in. apart on ungreased baking sheets. Using the end of a wooden spoon handle, make an indentation in the center of each. For filling, melt chocolate chips and condensed milk in a heavy saucepan over medium heat; stir until smooth. Stir in pecans, coconut and enough milk to achieve desired consistency. Spoon 1 teaspoon into each cookie. Bake at 350° for 8-10 minutes or until firm. Remove to wire racks to cool. **Yield:** 4 dozen.

Chocolate Mint Cookies

Cindy Ann Gray, Republic, Missouri

Of all my cookie recipes, these are my family's favorites. When they're given a choice between them and store-bought mint cookies, these win hands down.

3/4 cup butter (no substitutes)
1-1/2 cups packed dark brown sugar
2 tablespoons water
2 cups (12 ounces) semisweet chocolate chips
2 eggs
2-1/2 cups all-purpose flour
1-1/4 teaspoons baking soda
1/2 teaspoon salt
2 packages (4.67 ounces *each*) mint Andes
 candies, halved

In a heavy saucepan, combine butter, brown sugar and water; cook over low heat until butter is melted. Remove from the heat; stir in chips until melted. Transfer to a mixing bowl; cool for 10 minutes. Add eggs, one at a time, beating well after each addition. Combine flour, baking soda and salt; gradually add to the chocolate mixture. Cover and refrigerate for 1 hour or until easy to handle. Roll into 1-in. balls. Place 2 in. apart on ungreased baking sheets. Bake at 350° for 10-12 minutes or until surface cracks. Remove to wire racks. Immediately place half of a mint candy on each cookie. Let stand until candy begins to melt; spread with a knife. **Yield:** about 9 dozen.

Bars & Brownies

Cherry Coconut Bars

Marguerite Emery, Orland, California

(Pictured at left)

I came across these bars while stationed at a Michigan Air Force base in 1964 and have been making them ever since. My children don't think an event is special unless they are part of it.

    1 cup all-purpose flour
    3 tablespoons confectioners' sugar
1/2 cup cold butter (no substitutes)
FILLING:
    2 eggs
    1 cup sugar
    1 teaspoon vanilla extract
1/4 cup all-purpose flour
1/2 teaspoon baking powder
1/4 teaspoon salt
3/4 cup chopped walnuts
1/2 cup quartered maraschino cherries
1/2 cup flaked coconut

In a bowl, combine flour and confectioners' sugar; cut in butter until crumbly. Press into a lightly greased 13-in. x 9-in. x 2-in. baking pan. Bake at 350° for 10-12 minutes or until lightly browned. Cool on a wire rack. For filling, combine the eggs, sugar and vanilla in a bowl. Combine flour, baking powder and salt; add to the egg mixture. Stir in walnuts, cherries and coconut. Spread over crust. Bake for 20-25 minutes or until firm. Cool on a wire rack. Cut into bars. **Yield:** 3 dozen.

Lemon Shortbread Squares

Janet Sater, Arlington, Virginia

(Pictured at left)

During the Christmas season, I keep homemade cookies available in my office to share with co-workers. These easy-to-prepare squares always get rave reviews.

> **FRUIT-FILLED FLAVORS.** Pictured at left, clockwise from top: Cherry Coconut Bars, Lemon Shortbread Squares and Lattice Fruit Bars (all recipes on this page).

1/2 cup plus 2 tablespoons butter (no substitutes), softened
1/2 cup confectioners' sugar
1-1/4 cups all-purpose flour
1/2 teaspoon lemon extract
1/2 teaspoon vanilla extract
1/4 teaspoon grated lemon peel, optional
1/2 cup chopped pecans

In a mixing bowl, cream butter and sugar. Add flour and extracts. Mix until dough forms a ball and pulls away from the side of the bowl. Stir in lemon peel if desired. Press into an ungreased 9-in. square baking pan. Score with a sharp knife into 16 squares. Prick each square twice with a fork. Sprinkle with pecans; press firmly into dough. Bake at 325° for 20-25 minutes or until lightly browned and pecans are toasted. Cool for 5 minutes. Cut along scored lines. Cool completely in pan on a wire rack. Store in an airtight container. **Yield:** 16 squares.

Lattice Fruit Bars

Betty Keisling, Knoxville, Tennessee

(Pictured at left)

These attractive bars make a beautiful addition to any table. I like the fact that one batch goes a long way.

    3 cups all-purpose flour
    1 cup sugar
    1 teaspoon baking powder
1/2 teaspoon salt
    1 cup cold butter *or* margarine
    2 eggs
    2 teaspoons vanilla extract
3/4 cup apricot preserves
3/4 cup raspberry preserves

In a bowl, combine the flour, sugar, baking powder and salt; cut in butter until crumbly. Combine eggs and vanilla; add to crumb mixture until blended. Set aside one-fourth of the dough; cover and refrigerate for at least 45 minutes. Press remaining dough into an ungreased 15-in. x 10-in. x 1-in. baking pan. Spread 1/4 cup apricot preserves in a 1-3/4-in. strip over one long side of crust. Spread 1/4 cup of raspberry preserves in a 1-3/4-in. strip adjoining the apricot strip. Repeat twice. Roll out reserved dough to 1/8-in. thickness. Cut into 1/2-in. strips; make a lattice top. Bake at 325° for 30-35 minutes or until lightly browned. Cool on a wire rack. Cut into bars. **Yield:** about 3-1/2 dozen.

Peanut Butter Brownies

Kathy Crow, Payson, Arizona

Dressing up a boxed cake mix with peanut butter and melted chocolate chips is the secret to this super easy recipe. My daughter Delleen got this recipe from co-workers and then shared it with me.

    1 package (18-1/4 ounces) chocolate cake mix
1/3 cup vegetable oil
    1 egg
    1 can (14 ounces) sweetened condensed milk
    2 cups (12 ounces) semisweet chocolate chips, melted
1/2 cup peanut butter
    1 teaspoon vanilla extract

In a bowl, combine the cake mix, oil and egg until crumbly. Set aside 1 cup for topping. Firmly press remaining mixture into a greased 13-in. x 9-in. x 2-in. baking pan; set aside. In a bowl, combine the milk, chocolate, peanut butter and vanilla until smooth. Spread over crust. Sprinkle with reserved crumb mixture. Bake at 350° for 25-30 minutes or until brownies pull away from the pan. Cool on a wire rack. Cut into bars. **Yield:** 4-1/2 dozen.

Cinnamon Raisin Bars

Nancy Rohr, St. Louis, Missouri

Although these bars keep well, they don't last long with my husband around. As soon as the house fills with their wonderful aroma, he comes running!

1/2 cup butter *or* margarine, softened
    1 cup packed brown sugar
1-1/2 cups all-purpose flour
1-1/2 cups quick-cooking oats
1/2 teaspoon baking soda
1/2 teaspoon salt
    2 tablespoons water
RAISIN FILLING:
1/4 cup sugar
    1 tablespoon cornstarch
    1 cup water
    2 cups raisins
ICING:
    1 cup confectioners' sugar
1/4 teaspoon ground cinnamon
    1 to 2 tablespoons milk

In a mixing bowl, cream butter and brown sugar. Combine flour, oats, baking soda and salt; add to creamed mixture with water. Beat until crumbly.

Firmly press half into a greased 13-in. x 9-in. x 2-in. baking pan; set the remaining oat mixture aside. In a saucepan, combine the sugar, cornstarch and water until smooth; stir in raisins. Cook and stir over medium heat until thick and bubbly. Cool to room temperature; spread over crust. Top with reserved oat mixture and pat down. Bake at 350° for 30-35 minutes or until golden brown. Cool on a wire rack. In a small bowl, combine confectioners' sugar and cinnamon; stir in enough milk to reach drizzling consistency. Drizzle over bars. Cut and store in an airtight container. **Yield:** about 3 dozen.

Chewy Walnut Bars

Nancy Tuschak, Vacaville, California

Since they need just four ingredients and one bowl to dirty, I often whip up a batch of these family-favorite bars. I'm thanked "mmmm-many" times over!

2-1/3 cups packed brown sugar
    2 cups biscuit/baking mix
    4 eggs
    2 cups chopped walnuts

In a bowl, combine brown sugar and biscuit mix. Add eggs and beat well. Fold in the walnuts. Pour into a greased 13-in. x 9-in. x 2-in. baking pan. Bake at 350° for 30-35 minutes or until golden brown. Cool on a wire rack. Cut into bars. **Yield:** about 3 dozen.

Chocolate Caramel Bars

Judy Broody, Oak Forest, Illinois

These bars have a delightful combination of chocolate, caramel and walnuts. I often rely on bar cookies for their ease of preparation.

1/2 cup butter *or* margarine, softened
    1 cup packed brown sugar
    2 cups all-purpose flour
CARAMEL LAYER:
2/3 cup butter *or* margarine
1/2 cup packed brown sugar
    1 cup chopped walnuts
TOPPING:
1-1/2 cups semisweet chocolate chips

In a mixing bowl, cream butter and brown sugar. Add flour and mix well. Press into a greased 13-in. x 9-in. x 2-in. baking pan; set aside. In a saucepan, combine butter and brown sugar. Bring to a boil; cook for 1 minute. Stir in walnuts. Spread over crust.

Bake at 350° for 16-18 minutes or until set. Immediately sprinkle with chocolate chips. Allow chips to soften for a few minutes, then spread over caramel layer. Cool on a wire rack. Cut into bars. **Yield:** 3 dozen.

Chocolate Cheesecake Bars

Louise Good, Flemington, New Jersey

When you don't have time to bake a real cheesecake, reach for this tasty recipe. A thick, moist crust is covered with a creamy chocolate filling and then sprinkled with a crumb topping.

    1 cup butter *or* margarine, softened
1-1/2 cups sugar
    2 eggs
1/2 teaspoon almond extract
    3 cups all-purpose flour
    1 teaspoon baking powder
1/2 teaspoon salt
FILLING:
    2 cups (12 ounces) semisweet chocolate chips
    1 package (8 ounces) cream cheese
    1 can (5 ounces) evaporated milk
    1 cup chopped walnuts
1/2 teaspoon almond extract

In a mixing bowl, cream butter and sugar. Add eggs, one at a time, beating well after each addition. Beat in extract. Combine flour, baking powder and salt; gradually add to the creamed mixture until mixture resembles coarse crumbs (do not overmix). Set aside half for topping. Press the remaining crumb mixture into a greased 13-in. x 9-in. x 2-in. baking pan. For filling, combine the chocolate chips, cream cheese and milk in a saucepan. Cook over low heat until chips are melted; stir until smooth and blended. Remove from the heat; stir in walnuts and extract. Spread over crust; sprinkle with reserved crumb mixture. Bake at 375° for 35-40 minutes or until golden brown. Cool on a wire rack. Cut into bars. **Yield:** 4 dozen.

Very Chocolate Brownies

Jan Mock, Dillon, Montana

These brownies have chocolate chips and melted chocolate in the batter, making them doubly delicious. It's a crowd-pleasing treat I can always count on.

2/3 cup butter *or* margarine
1-1/2 cups sugar

1/4 cup water
    4 cups (24 ounces) semisweet chocolate chips, *divided*
    2 teaspoons vanilla extract
    4 eggs
1-1/2 cups all-purpose flour
1/2 teaspoon baking soda
1/2 teaspoon salt

In a heavy saucepan, bring butter, sugar and water to a boil, stirring constantly. Remove from the heat. Stir in 2 cups of chocolate chips until melted; cool slightly. Beat in vanilla. In a mixing bowl, beat eggs. Gradually add chocolate mixture; mix well. Combine the flour, baking soda and salt; gradually add to chocolate mixture. Stir in remaining chocolate chips. Spread into a greased 13-in. x 9-in. x 2-in. baking pan. Bake at 325° for 35-40 minutes or until a toothpick inserted near the center comes out clean. Cool on a wire rack. Cut into bars. **Yield:** 3 dozen.

Double Chip Meringue Bars

Dawn Onuffer, Freeport, Florida

This recipe came from my mom. It originally called just for chocolate chips, but the addition of peanut butter chips was a huge success. And the meringue topping makes these bars extra special

    1 cup butter *or* margarine, melted
1/2 cup sugar
1/2 cup packed brown sugar
    2 egg yolks
    1 teaspoon water
    1 teaspoon vanilla extract
    2 cups all-purpose flour
    1 teaspoon baking powder
1/4 teaspoon baking soda
1/4 teaspoon salt
    1 cup semisweet chocolate chips
    1 cup peanut butter chips
TOPPING:
    2 egg whites
    1 cup packed brown sugar

In a mixing bowl, cream butter and sugars. Beat in the egg yolks, water and vanilla; mix well. Combine the next four ingredients; gradually add to creamed mixture. Spread into a greased 13-in. x 9-in. x 2-in. baking pan. Sprinkle with chips and pat lightly. For topping, beat egg whites until stiff peaks form. Gradually add brown sugar and mix well. Spread evenly over chips. Bake at 350° for 25-30 minutes or until golden brown. Cool on a wire rack. Cut into bars. Store in the refrigerator. **Yield:** 4 dozen.

Cream Cheese Brownies

Carolyn Reed, North Robinson, Ohio

A friend from church shared this recipe with me. Cream cheese lends itself to a moist and chewy bar that's finger-lickin' good!

> 2 packages (8 ounces *each*) cream cheese, softened
> 2 cups sugar, *divided*
> 3 tablespoons milk
> 1 cup butter *or* margarine, softened
> 2/3 cup instant hot cocoa mix*
> 4 eggs
> 2 teaspoons vanilla extract
> 1-1/2 cups all-purpose flour
> 1 cup chopped nuts

In a small mixing bowl, beat cream cheese, 1/2 cup sugar and milk until fluffy; set aside. In a large mixing bowl, cream the butter, hot cocoa mix and remaining sugar. Beat in eggs and vanilla. Stir in flour and nuts; pour half into a greased 13-in. x 9-in. x 2-in. baking pan. Spread with the cream cheese mixture. Top with remaining batter. Cut through batter with a knife to swirl the cream cheese. Bake at 350° for 35-40 minutes or until a toothpick inserted near the center comes out clean. Cool on a wire rack. Cut into bars. **Yield:** 2-1/2 dozen. ***Editor's Note:** This recipe was tested with Swiss Miss instant cocoa.

Coconut Pecan Bars

Susan Hamilton, Fulton, Missouri

With a butterscotch flavor, these tasty bars have always been welcomed with open arms by my family. Since they're simple to make, kids can have fun pitching in.

> 1 cup butter *or* margarine, softened
> 2 cups packed brown sugar
> 2 eggs
> 2 teaspoons vanilla extract
> 2 cups all-purpose flour
> 1 teaspoon salt
> 1 teaspoon baking powder
> 1-1/2 cups flaked coconut
> 1 cup chopped pecans
> Confectioners' sugar

In a mixing bowl, cream butter and brown sugar. Add eggs, one at a time, beating well after each addition. Beat in vanilla. Combine flour, salt and baking powder; gradually add to the creamed mixture. Stir in coconut and pecans (batter will be thick). Spread into a greased 15-in. x 10-in. x 1-in. baking pan. Bake at

350° for 20-25 minutes or until a toothpick inserted near the center comes out clean. Cool on a wire rack. Dust with confectioners' sugar. Cut into bars. **Yield:** 4 dozen.

Cheesecake Dreams

Barbara Allstrand, Oceanside, California

These bars are a "dream" not only because of their creamy filling but for their ease of preparation. Cheesecake lovers can't eat just one!

> 1 cup all-purpose flour
> 1/3 cup packed brown sugar
> 1/2 cup chopped pecans
> 1/3 cup butter *or* margarine, melted
> **FILLING:**
> 1 package (8 ounces) cream cheese, softened
> 1/4 cup sugar
> 1 egg
> 2 tablespoons milk
> 1 tablespoon lemon juice
> 1 teaspoon vanilla extract

In a bowl, combine the flour, brown sugar and pecans. Stir in butter; mix well. Set aside 1/3 cup for topping. Press remaining mixture into a greased 8-in. square baking pan. Bake at 350° for 12-15 minutes or until lightly browned. Meanwhile, in a mixing bowl, beat cream cheese and sugar. Beat in the egg, milk, lemon juice and vanilla. Pour over crust; sprinkle with reserved pecan mixture. Bake for 20-25 minutes or until firm. Cool on a wire rack. Cut into 16 squares, then cut each square in half diagonally. Store in the refrigerator. **Yield:** 32 bars.

Chewy Spice Bars

Cassie Vetsch, Los Lunas, New Mexico

I first sampled these bars when a student's mother brought them in for a party at the school where I taught. I enjoyed them so much I had to get the recipe.

> 1 cup butter *or* margarine, softened
> 1-1/2 cups sugar
> 1 cup packed brown sugar
> 2 eggs
> 1 tablespoon milk
> 1-1/2 teaspoons vanilla extract
> 3 cups quick-cooking oats
> 1-1/2 cups all-purpose flour
> 1-1/4 teaspoons baking soda
> 1 teaspoon salt
> 1/2 to 1 teaspoon ground cinnamon
> 1/4 teaspoon ground mace

1/4 teaspoon ground nutmeg
1/8 teaspoon ground cloves
2 cups (12 ounces) semisweet chocolate chips
1-1/4 cups flaked coconut
1 cup chopped walnuts
1 cup cornflakes

In a mixing bowl, cream butter and sugars. Add the eggs, one at a time, beating well after each addition. Beat in milk and vanilla. Combine oats, flour, baking soda, salt, cinnamon, mace, nutmeg and cloves; gradually add to creamed mixture. Stir in the remaining ingredients. Spread into a greased 15-in. x 10-in. x 1-in. baking pan. Bake at 375° for 25-30 minutes or until golden brown. Cool on a wire rack. Cut into bars. **Yield:** about 5 dozen.

Peppermint Crumb Squares

Martha Kerr, Abilene, Texas

Although I have a boxful of recipes, I often opt to make up my own. My granddaughter likes to eat these bars when she visits.

3/4 cup butter *or* margarine, softened
1/2 cup packed brown sugar
2 cups all-purpose flour
1 can (14 ounces) sweetened condensed milk
1 package (11 ounces) vanilla chips
2/3 cup crushed peppermint candy

In a mixing bowl, cream butter and brown sugar. Add flour; beat until crumbly. Press 2 cups into a greased 13-in. x 9-in. x 2-in. baking pan; set remaining crumb mixture aside. Bake the crust at 350° for 8-10 minutes. Meanwhile, in a microwave or double boiler, heat milk and vanilla chips until chips are melted; stir until smooth. Pour over hot crust and spread until smooth. Combine candy and reserved crumb mixture; sprinkle over top. Bake for 18-22 minutes or until lightly browned. Cool on a wire rack. Cut into squares. **Yield:** 4 dozen.

Blonde Brownies

Anne Weiler, Philadelphia, Pennsylvania

My family has enjoyed these bars as a potluck dessert, brown-bag treat and anytime snack many times throughout the years. Butterscotch or peanut butter chips can be used in place of the chocolate chips.

1/4 cup butter-flavored shortening
1-1/2 cups packed brown sugar
2 eggs
1/2 teaspoon vanilla extract

1 cup all-purpose flour
1-1/2 teaspoons baking powder
1/2 teaspoon salt
1 cup chopped walnuts
1/2 cup semisweet chocolate chips

In a mixing bowl, cream shortening and brown sugar. Add eggs, one at a time, beating well after each addition. Beat in vanilla. Combine flour, baking powder and salt; gradually add to the creamed mixture. Stir in nuts and chocolate chips. Spread into a greased 11-in. x 7-in. x 2-in. baking pan. Bake at 350° for 25-30 minutes or until a toothpick inserted near the center comes out clean. Cool on a wire rack. Cut into bars. **Yield:** 2 dozen.

Chocolaty Raisin Oat Bars

Linda Ploeg, Rockford, Michigan

These attractive layered bars have a similar taste to chocolate-covered raisins. "Yum!" is usually how folks describe every bite.

1 can (14 ounces) sweetened condensed milk
2 squares (1 ounce *each*) unsweetened chocolate
2 cups raisins
1 cup butter *or* margarine, softened
1-1/3 cups packed brown sugar
1-1/2 teaspoons vanilla extract
2-1/2 cups quick-cooking oats
2 cups all-purpose flour
3/4 teaspoon salt
1/2 teaspoon baking soda

In a microwave-safe bowl, combine milk and chocolate. Microwave on high for 2 minutes or until chocolate is melted; stir until smooth. Stir in raisins; set aside to cool slightly. In a mixing bowl, cream butter and brown sugar. Beat in vanilla. Combine the remaining ingredients; gradually add to creamed mixture (dough will be crumbly). Set aside half for topping. Press remaining crumb mixture into an ungreased 13-in. x 9-in. x 2-in. baking pan. Spread with the chocolate raisin mixture. Sprinkle with reserved crumb mixture; press down lightly. Bake at 375° for 25-30 minutes or until golden brown. Cool on a wire rack. Cut into bars. **Yield:** 4 dozen. **Editor's Note:** This recipe was tested in a 900-watt microwave.

TO EASILY CRUSH peppermint candy, place the candy pieces in a resealable plastic bag; seal. Pound the candies with a meat mallet or hammer on a sturdy countertop.

Spicy Butter Thins

Elsie Vince, Peoria, Arizona

I spotted this recipe in a newspaper when teaching in California more than 20 years ago. Even today, my son says these are his all-time favorite treat.

- **3/4 cup all-purpose flour**
- **1/4 cup sugar**
- **1 teaspoon ground cinnamon**
- **1 teaspoon instant coffee granules**
- **1/2 teaspoon ground ginger**
- **1/2 cup butter *or* margarine**
- **1 cup butterscotch chips, *divided***
- **1 egg**
- **1/2 cup chopped salted peanuts**

In a bowl, combine the first five ingredients; set aside. In a heavy saucepan over low heat, melt butter and 2/3 cup butterscotch chips. Remove from the heat. Stir in the dry ingredients and egg; mix well. Spread into an ungreased 15-in. x 10-in. x 1-in. baking pan. Sprinkle with peanuts and remaining chips. Bake at 300° for 25-30 minutes or until lightly browned. Immediately cut into bars and remove from pan. Cool on wire racks. Store in an airtight container. **Yield:** about 3 dozen.

Frosted Cherry Nut Bars

Christine Carter, Corinth, Vermont

Cherries, nuts and chocolate chips peek out of these bars, making them impossible for folks to stop at trying just one. With their pretty look, they're especially nice to have on hand during the holidays.

- **1/2 cup butter (no substitutes), softened**
- **1/2 cup sugar**
- **1/2 cup packed brown sugar**
- **2 eggs**
- **1 teaspoon vanilla extract**
- **2 cups all-purpose flour**
- **1-1/2 teaspoons baking powder**
- **1/2 teaspoon salt**
- **3/4 cup milk**
- **1 cup mixed nuts, coarsely chopped**
- **1 cup halved maraschino cherries**
- **1 cup (6 ounces) semisweet chocolate chips**
- **FROSTING:**
- **1/4 cup butter (no substitutes)**
- **2 tablespoons milk**
- **1/2 teaspoon vanilla extract**
- **2 cups confectioners' sugar**

In a mixing bowl, cream butter and sugars. Add eggs,

one at a time, beating well after each addition. Beat in vanilla. Combine the flour, baking powder and salt; add to creamed mixture alternately with milk. Stir in nuts, cherries and chocolate chips. Spread into a greased 15-in. x 10-in. x 1-in. baking pan. Bake at 325° for 25-30 minutes or until golden brown. Meanwhile, in a saucepan over medium heat, melt butter until golden brown, about 7 minutes. Add milk and vanilla. Remove from the heat; beat in confectioners' sugar until smooth. Frost warm bars. Cool on a wire rack before cutting. **Yield:** about 6 dozen.

Peanut Butter 'n' Chocolate Bars

Debra Rowley, Hattiesburg, Mississippi

This is my most requested recipe. Folks especially seem to like the fact they can be creative by varying the ingredients. For instance, I sometimes replace the chocolate or peanut butter chips with butterscotch chips.

- **1 cup butter *or* margarine, softened**
- **3/4 cup sugar**
- **3/4 cup packed brown sugar**
- **2 eggs**
- **1 teaspoon vanilla extract**
- **2-1/4 cups all-purpose flour**
- **1 teaspoon baking soda**
- **1/4 teaspoon salt**
- **1-1/4 cups semisweet chocolate chips**
- **1-1/4 cups peanut butter chips**

In a mixing bowl, cream butter and sugars. Add the eggs, one at a time, beating well after each addition. Beat in vanilla. Combine the flour, baking soda and salt; gradually add to creamed mixture. Stir in chips. Spread into a greased 15-in. x 10-in. x 1-in. baking pan. Bake at 375° for 20-25 or until a toothpick inserted near the center comes out clean. Cool on a wire rack. Cut into bars. **Yield:** about 4 dozen.

Fudge Walnut Brownies

Donna Nannenga, Wheatfield, Indiana

I've tried numerous brownie recipes, but this recipe is the best by far. A well-known baker in our town generously shared the recipe with me.

- **1-1/4 cups butter *or* margarine, softened**
- **4 cups sugar**
- **8 eggs**
- **2 teaspoons vanilla extract**
- **2 cups all-purpose flour**
- **1-1/4 cups baking cocoa**
- **1 teaspoon salt**
- **2 cups chopped walnuts**

FROSTING:
    1/2 cup butter *or* margarine
    6 tablespoons milk
    3 tablespoons baking cocoa
3-1/2 cups confectioners' sugar
    1 teaspoon vanilla extract
Additional chopped walnuts, optional

In a mixing bowl, cream butter and sugar. Add eggs, one at a time, beating well after each addition. Beat in vanilla. Combine the flour, cocoa and salt; gradually add to creamed mixture. Stir in walnuts. Spread into a greased 15-in. x 10-in. x 1-in. baking pan. Bake at 325° for 40-45 minutes or until top springs back when lightly touched. Meanwhile, melt butter in a saucepan over low heat. Remove from the heat; stir in milk and cocoa until smooth. Return to the heat and bring to a boil; boil for 4 minutes, stirring constantly. Remove from the heat; add confectioners' sugar and vanilla. Mix well. Frost warm brownies. Sprinkle with walnuts if desired. Cool on a wire rack before cutting. **Yield:** 5 dozen.

Gold Rush Brownies

Kellie Erwin, Westerville, Ohio

With six kids to keep an eye on, my mother relied on quick-and-easy recipes like this. Now my own family, who doesn't usually care for nuts, can't resist these chewy brownies.

    2 cups graham cracker crumbs (about 32 squares)
    1 cup (6 ounces) semisweet chocolate chips
1/2 cup chopped pecans
    1 can (14 ounces) sweetened condensed milk

In a bowl, combine the crumbs, chocolate chips and pecans. Stir in milk until blended (batter will be stiff). Spread into a greased 8-in. square baking pan. Bake at 350° for 25-30 minutes or until a toothpick inserted near the center comes out clean. Cool on a wire rack. Cut into bars. **Yield:** 1 dozen.

Frosted Cocoa Bars

Cathryn White, Newark, Delaware

It's nice to have a trusty bar recipe like this when you are short on time. The subtle coffee flavor in the frosting adds a tasty touch.

1-1/4 cups shortening
1-1/4 cups packed brown sugar
    1/2 cup corn syrup
1-1/2 teaspoons vanilla extract

    4 eggs
1-1/4 cups all-purpose flour
    2/3 cup baking cocoa
    1 teaspoon salt
FROSTING:
    1/2 cup butter (no substitutes)
    3 cups confectioners' sugar
    2 tablespoons brewed coffee
1-1/2 teaspoons vanilla extract
    3 to 4 tablespoons milk

In a mixing bowl, cream shortening and brown sugar. Beat in corn syrup and vanilla. Add eggs, one at a time, beating well after each addition. Combine flour, cocoa and salt; gradually add to creamed mixture. Spread into a greased 15-in. x 10-in. x 1-in. baking pan. Bake at 350° for 20-25 minutes or until a toothpick inserted near the center comes out clean. Cool on a wire rack. In a large saucepan over medium heat, melt butter until golden brown, about 7 minutes. Remove from the heat. Stir in sugar, coffee, vanilla and enough milk until frosting reaches spreading consistency. Frost cooled brownies. Cover and refrigerate until firm, about 1 hour, before cutting. **Yield:** 8 dozen.

Chocolate Bliss Brownies

Juanita Lou Williams, Enid, Oklahoma

I first tried these at a brunch and begged the hostess for the recipe. Sometimes I'll eliminate the frosting and just sprinkle the top with confectioners' sugar.

    1/2 cup butter *or* margarine, softened
    1 cup sugar
    4 eggs
    1 can (16 ounces) chocolate syrup
    1 cup all-purpose flour
    1 cup chopped nuts
    1 teaspoon salt
FROSTING:
    6 tablespoons butter *or* margarine
1-1/2 cups sugar
    1/3 cup milk
    1/2 cup semisweet chocolate chips

In a mixing bowl, cream the butter and sugar. Add eggs, one at a time, beating well after each addition. Add chocolate syrup. Beat in flour, nuts and salt until blended. Pour into a greased 13-in. x 9-in. x 2-in. baking pan. Bake at 350° for 25-30 minutes or until a toothpick inserted near the center comes out clean (brownies may appear moist). Cool on a wire rack. In a saucepan, melt butter. Add sugar and milk. Bring to a boil; boil for 30 seconds. Remove from the heat; stir in the chips until melted. Beat until frosting reaches spreading consistency. Frost cooled brownies; cut. **Yield:** 4-1/2 dozen.

Final Exam Brownies

Phyllis Crawford, Natrona Heights, Pennsylvania

(Pictured at left)

When my daughter was in college, she kept a batch of these fudgy brownies around when studying for final exams. With a blend of chocolate chips, marshmallows and nuts, they always earn high marks!

- 4 squares (1 ounce *each*) unsweetened chocolate
- 1 cup butter (no substitutes)
- 2 cups sugar
- 4 eggs
- 1 teaspoon vanilla extract
- 1 cup all-purpose flour
- 2 cups miniature marshmallows
- 1 cup chopped pecans *or* walnuts
- 1-1/2 cups semisweet chocolate chips, *divided*

In a microwave or double boiler, melt unsweetened chocolate and butter; stir until smooth. In a mixing bowl, combine the sugar, eggs, vanilla and chocolate mixture. Add flour; mix well. Fold in marshmallows, nuts and 1/2 cup chocolate chips. Spread into a greased 13-in. x 9-in. x 2-in. baking pan. Sprinkle with remaining chocolate chips. Bake at 350° for 40-45 minutes or until top is set. Cool on a wire rack. Cut into bars. **Yield:** 2-1/2 dozen.

WHEN MAILING bar cookies, wrap bars in pairs (flat sides together) in plastic wrap or foil. Pack them close together so they won't have room to move around and break. Unfrosted bars are the best for mailing.

Peppermint Chocolate Bars

Christine Harrell, Chester, Virginia

(Pictured at left)

I received this treasured recipe from a dear friend years ago. The frosting and topping make these thin brownies eye-catching.

- 1/2 cup butter (no substitutes)
- 2 squares (1 ounce *each*) unsweetened chocolate
- 2 eggs

BACK TO BASICS. Pictured at left, clockwise from top: Final Exam Brownies, Apricot Squares and Peppermint Chocolate Bars (all recipes on this page).

- 1 cup sugar
- 2 teaspoons vanilla extract
- 1/2 cup all-purpose flour
- 1/2 teaspoon salt
- 1/2 cup chopped pecans *or* walnuts

FROSTING:
- 1/4 cup butter (no substitutes), softened
- 2 cups confectioners' sugar
- 1 teaspoon peppermint extract
- 3 to 4 tablespoons whipping cream

TOPPING:
- 1 square (1 ounce) semisweet chocolate
- 1 tablespoon butter (no substitutes)

In a microwave or double boiler, melt butter and chocolate; cool slightly. In a mixing bowl, beat the eggs, sugar and vanilla. Add the chocolate mixture and mix well. Combine flour and salt; gradually add to chocolate mixture. Stir in nuts. Spread into a greased 13-in. x 9-in. x 2-in. baking pan. Bake at 350° for 16-20 minutes or until a toothpick inserted near the center comes out clean. Cool on a wire rack. In a mixing bowl, cream butter, sugar and extract. Add enough cream until frosting reaches spreading consistency. Frost cooled bars. Melt chocolate and butter; drizzle over frosting. Cut into bars. **Yield:** 4 dozen.

Apricot Squares

Pat Ruggiero, Okemos, Michigan

(Pictured at left)

I remember my mom making these fruity bars for PTA meetings when I was in elementary school more than 40 years ago. Now I serve these bars for a variety of functions.

- 1 cup butter *or* margarine, softened
- 1 cup sugar
- 1 egg
- 1 teaspoon lemon extract
- 3 cups all-purpose flour
- 4 teaspoons grated orange peel
- 1 teaspoon baking powder
- 1/4 teaspoon salt

FILLING:
- 1 jar (18 ounces) apricot preserves
- 2 teaspoons lemon juice
- 1 teaspoon grated lemon peel

In a mixing bowl, cream butter and sugar. Add egg and extract; mix well. Combine the flour, orange peel, baking powder and salt; gradually add to creamed mixture. Set aside one-third for the topping. Press remaining dough into a greased 13-in. x 9-in. x 2-in. baking pan. Combine preserves, lemon juice and peel; spread evenly over crust. Crumble reserved dough over filling. Bake at 350° for 40 minutes or until golden brown. Cool on a wire rack. Cut into squares. **Yield:** 2 dozen.

Raspberry Delights

Georgiana Hagman, Louisville, Kentucky

These attractive bars have a rich buttery crust holding the sweet jam topping. They're a big favorite on my Christmas cookie trays.

1 cup butter (no substitutes), softened
1 cup sugar
2 egg yolks
2 cups all-purpose flour
1 cup coarsely ground pecans
1 cup raspberry jam

In a mixing bowl, cream butter and sugar. Add egg yolks; mix well. Gradually add flour. Stir in the pecans. Spread half into a lightly greased 13-in. x 9-in. x 2-in. baking pan. Top with jam. Drop remaining dough by teaspoonfuls over jam. Bake at 350° for 25-30 minutes or until top is golden brown. Cool on a wire rack. Cut into bars. **Yield:** 3 dozen.

Frosted Cinnamon Zucchini Bars

Bonita Holzbacher, Batesville, Indiana

I figure you can never have enough recipes calling for zucchini! These cake-like bars with a cinnamon-flavored frosting are unbelievably good.

3/4 cup butter *or* margarine, softened
1/2 cup sugar
1/2 cup packed brown sugar
2 eggs
1 teaspoon vanilla extract
1-3/4 cups all-purpose flour
1-1/2 teaspoons baking powder
2 cups shredded zucchini
1 cup flaked coconut
3/4 cup chopped walnuts
FROSTING:
2 cups confectioners' sugar
1 teaspoon ground cinnamon
2 tablespoons butter *or* margarine, melted
1 teaspoon vanilla extract
2 to 3 tablespoons milk

In a mixing bowl, cream butter and sugars. Add the eggs, one at a time, beating well after each addition. Beat in vanilla. Combine flour and baking powder; gradually add to the creamed mixture. Stir in zucchini, coconut and nuts. Spread into a greased 15-in. x 10-in. x 1-in. baking pan. Bake at 350° for 25-30 minutes or until a toothpick inserted near the center comes out clean. Cool on a wire rack. In a bowl, combine sugar and cinnamon. Stir in butter, vanilla and enough milk until frosting reaches spreading consistency. Frost cooled bars; cut. **Yield:** about 5 dozen.

Fudgy Brownies

Dorothy Scalzitti, Stanwood, Washington

I love to cook and look forward to spending quality time with my young son in the kitchen. This is one recipe I'll be sure to share with him when he gets older.

2 cups sugar
3/4 cup baking cocoa
1/2 teaspoon baking soda
2/3 cup vegetable oil, *divided*
1/2 cup boiling water
1-1/3 cups all-purpose flour
1 teaspoon vanilla extract
1/4 teaspoon salt
2 eggs
1 cup chopped walnuts

In a mixing bowl, combine the sugar, cocoa and baking soda. Add 1/3 cup oil and water; beat until smooth. Beat in the flour, vanilla, salt, eggs and remaining oil. Stir in walnuts. Spread into a greased 13-in. x 9-in. x 2-in. baking pan. Bake at 350° for 35-40 minutes or until a toothpick inserted near the center comes out clean. Cool on a wire rack. Cut into bars. **Yield:** 6 dozen.

Chewy Pecan Bars

Jeanne Gerlach, Frisco, Colorado

A friend from Texas gave me this recipe years ago. Because it's so easy to make, I've relied on it quite often.

1/4 cup butter *or* margarine, melted
4 eggs
2 cups packed brown sugar
2 teaspoons vanilla extract
2/3 cup all-purpose flour
1/4 teaspoon baking soda
1/4 teaspoon salt
2 cups chopped pecans
Confectioners' sugar

Spread butter evenly in an ungreased 13-in. x 9-in. x 2-in. baking pan. In a mixing bowl, beat eggs, brown sugar and vanilla. Combine flour, baking soda and salt; gradually add to egg mixture. Stir in pecans. Spread into prepared pan. Bake at 350° for 30-35 minutes or until browned. Dust with confectioners' sugar. Cool on a wire rack. Cut into bars. **Yield:** 3 dozen.

Cool Lime Squares

TerryAnn Moore, Oaklyn, New Jersey

Folks always seem to enjoy this variation on the popular lemon bars. Lime juice adds fresh flavor while nuts add some crunch. They're especially refreshing during the warm summer months.

> 1 cup butter *or* margarine, melted
> 2 cups all-purpose flour
> 1/2 cup confectioners' sugar
> 1/2 cup ground almonds
> FILLING:
> 4 eggs
> 2 cups sugar
> 1/3 cup lime juice
> 1/4 cup all-purpose flour
> 1 teaspoon baking powder
> 1/2 teaspoon grated lime peel
> 1 to 2 drops green food coloring, optional
> 1/2 cup sliced almonds
> Confectioners' sugar

In a mixing bowl, combine the first four ingredients; mix well. Press into a greased 13-in. x 9-in. x 2-in. baking pan. Bake at 350° for 13-15 minutes or just until edges are lightly browned. Meanwhile, in a mixing bowl, combine eggs, sugar, lime juice, flour, baking powder, lime peel and food coloring if desired; beat until frothy. Pour over hot crust. Sprinkle with almonds. Bake for 20-25 minutes or until light golden brown. Cool on a wire rack. Dust with confectioners' sugar. Cut into squares. **Yield:** 4 dozen.

Chocolate Chip Marshmallow Bars

Sara Yoder, Apple Creek, Ohio

With marshmallows and chocolate chips, these melt-in-your-mouth bars appeal to kids of all ages. They disappear fast wherever I take them.

> 1 cup shortening
> 3/4 cup sugar
> 3/4 cup packed brown sugar
> 2 eggs
> 1 teaspoon vanilla extract
> 2-1/4 cups all-purpose flour
> 1 teaspoon baking soda
> 1 teaspoon salt
> 2 cups miniature marshmallows
> 1-1/2 cups semisweet chocolate chips
> 3/4 cup chopped walnuts

In a mixing bowl, cream shortening and sugars. Add eggs, one at a time, beating well after each addition. Beat in vanilla. Combine the flour, baking soda and salt; gradually add to creamed mixture. Stir in marshmallows, chips and walnuts. Spread into a greased 13-in. x 9-in. x 2-in. baking pan. Bake at 350° for 25-30 minutes or until golden brown. Cool on a wire rack. Cut into bars. **Yield:** 3 dozen.

Double-Decker Brownies

Mrs. Duane Adams, Soldiers Grove, Wisconsin

I love to take the grandchildren searching for walnuts in the woods around our house. These bars are real people pleasers, especially among men.

> 1 cup butter (no substitutes), softened
> 2 cups packed brown sugar
> 3 eggs
> 2 teaspoons vanilla extract
> 2 cups all-purpose flour
> 1-1/2 teaspoons baking powder
> 1/2 teaspoon salt
> 1 cup chopped walnuts
> 2 squares (1 ounce *each*) unsweetened chocolate, melted
> FROSTING:
> 1/4 cup butter (no substitutes)
> 2 squares (1 ounce *each*) unsweetened chocolate
> 2 cups confectioners' sugar
> 1-1/2 teaspoons vanilla extract
> 2 to 3 tablespoons milk

In a mixing bowl, cream butter and brown sugar. Add eggs, one at a time, beating well after each addition. Beat in vanilla. Combine the flour, baking powder and salt; gradually add to creamed mixture. Stir in walnuts. Divide batter in half. Stir chocolate into one portion; spread into a greased 13-in. x 9-in. x 2-in. baking pan. Spread remaining batter evenly over top. Bake at 350° for 30-35 minutes or until brownies begin to pull away from sides of pan. Cool on a wire rack. In a saucepan, melt butter and chocolate. Remove from the heat. Stir in confectioners' sugar, vanilla and enough milk to reach spreading consistency. Frost cooled brownies; cut. **Yield:** 3 dozen.

TO CUT BARS like a pro, line the baking pan with foil, leaving 3 inches hanging over each end. Grease the foil if the recipe instructs. Once the bars are baked and cooled, use the foil to lift the bars out. Cut into bars and discard foil. This not only makes it easier to cut the bars and saves cleanup time, it prevents your pans from getting scratched.

Caramel Pecan Bars

Emma Manning, Crossett, Arkansas

This recipe won first place at a cookie contest held where I work. These rich bars really capture the flavor of pecan pie.

1 cup butter *or* margarine
2-1/4 cups packed brown sugar
2 eggs
2 teaspoons vanilla extract
1-1/2 cups all-purpose flour
2 teaspoons baking powder
2 cups chopped pecans
Confectioners' sugar, optional

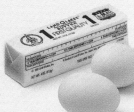

In a saucepan, heat butter and brown sugar over medium heat until sugar is dissolved. In a mixing bowl, combine the eggs, vanilla and butter mixture. Combine flour and baking powder; gradually add to the butter mixture. Stir in pecans. Spread into a greased 13-in. x 9-in. x 2-in. baking pan. Bake at 350° for 20-25 minutes or until a toothpick inserted near the center comes out with moist crumbs and edges are crisp. Cool on a wire rack. Dust with confectioners' sugar if desired. Cut into bars. **Yield:** 4 dozen.

Chocolate Cinnamon Squares

Keith Carlen, Ione, California

I thank my mom for stirring my interest in cooking and baking. Of all her treasured recipe cards I have, this is an all-time favorite.

1/2 cup butter *or* margarine, softened
1/2 cup shortening
1 cup sugar
1 egg plus 1 egg yolk
2 cups all-purpose flour
1 tablespoon ground cinnamon
1 teaspoon baking powder
1/2 teaspoon salt
TOPPING:
1 egg white
1 cup (6 ounces) semisweet chocolate chips
1/2 cup chopped walnuts
1/3 cup sugar
1 teaspoon ground cinnamon

In a mixing bowl, cream butter, shortening and sugar. Beat in egg and yolk. Combine flour, cinnamon, baking powder and salt; gradually add to creamed mixture. Spread into a greased 15-in. x 10-in. x 1-in. baking pan. Beat egg white until foamy; brush over

dough. Combine chocolate chips, nuts, sugar and cinnamon; sprinkle over dough. Bake at 350° for 25-30 minutes or until golden brown. Cool on a wire rack. Cut into squares. **Yield:** about 3 dozen.

Scotch Shortbread Bars

Jane Hodge, West End, North Carolina

It was at my bridal shower in 1960 that I first sampled these pretty bars. Now each time I make them, I'm reminded of that happy occasion.

1 cup butter (no substitutes), softened
1/2 cup confectioners' sugar
2 cups all-purpose flour
1/4 teaspoon baking powder
1/4 teaspoon salt
Additional confectioners' sugar

In a mixing bowl, cream butter and sugar. Combine flour, baking powder and salt; gradually add to the creamed mixture. Spread into an ungreased 11-in. x 7-in. x 2-in. baking pan. Prick several times with a fork. Bake at 350° for 20-22 minutes or until edges begin to brown. Dust with confectioners' sugar. Cool on a wire rack. Cut into bars. **Yield:** 2 dozen.

Three-Layer Chocolate Brownies

Billie Hopkins, Enterprise, Oregon

I often serve these hearty, cake-like brownies with a fork for easier eating. The oatmeal crust, fudgy filling and chocolate frosting make them a hit wherever I take them.

1 cup quick-cooking oats
1/2 cup packed brown sugar
1/3 cup all-purpose flour
1/4 teaspoon baking soda
1/4 teaspoon salt
1/4 cup butter (no substitutes), melted
FILLING:
1/2 cup butter (no substitutes)
2 squares (1 ounce *each*) semisweet chocolate
1 cup sugar
2 eggs, beaten
1/4 cup milk
2 teaspoons vanilla extract
2/3 cup all-purpose flour
1/4 teaspoon baking soda
1/4 teaspoon salt
FROSTING:
3 tablespoons butter (no substitutes), softened

Bars & Brownies

1 square (1 ounce) unsweetened chocolate,
   melted
1 cup confectioners' sugar
1 tablespoon milk
3/4 teaspoon vanilla extract

In a mixing bowl, combine the first six ingredients; beat on low speed until blended. Press into a greased 9-in. square baking pan. Bake at 350° for 10 minutes. Meanwhile, in a saucepan over low heat, melt butter and chocolate. Remove from the heat; stir in sugar, eggs, milk and vanilla. Combine flour, baking soda and salt; gradually add to the chocolate mixture and stir until smooth. Pour over crust. Bake for 35-40 minutes or until the top springs back when lightly touched. Cool on a wire rack. In a mixing bowl, combine frosting ingredients; beat until smooth. Frost cooled brownies; cut. **Yield:** 1-1/2 dozen.

Championship Chocolate Chip Bars

Cheryl Costello, Festus, Missouri

As the name suggests, you'll earn rave reviews next time these bars make an appearance on your table. Don't forget to have copies of the recipe on hand!

1-1/2 cups all-purpose flour
  1/2 cup packed brown sugar
  1/2 cup cold butter *or* margarine
    2 cups (12 ounces) semisweet chocolate chips,
    divided
    1 can (14 ounces) sweetened condensed milk
    1 egg
    1 teaspoon vanilla extract
    1 cup chopped walnuts

In a bowl, combine flour and brown sugar; cut in butter until crumbly. Stir in 1/2 cup chocolate chips. Press firmly into a greased 13-in. x 9-in. x 2-in. baking pan. Bake at 350° for 15 minutes. Meanwhile, combine milk, egg, vanilla, walnuts and remaining chips. Spread evenly over hot crust. Bake for 20-25 minutes or until light golden brown. Cool on a wire rack. Cut into bars. **Yield:** about 2-1/2 dozen.

Pumpkin Cheesecake Bars

Agnes Jasa, Malabar, Florida

This recipe caught my eye and was extremely popular at the annual Christmas party sponsored by our Extension Homemakers. It's a great dessert for fall.

  1 cup all-purpose flour
1/3 cup packed brown sugar

5 tablespoons cold butter *or* margarine
1 cup finely chopped pecans
1 package (8 ounces) cream cheese, softened
3/4 cup sugar
1/2 cup cooked *or* canned pumpkin
  2 eggs
1 teaspoon vanilla extract
1-1/2 teaspoons ground cinnamon
1 teaspoon ground allspice

In a bowl, combine flour and brown sugar. Cut in butter until crumbly. Stir in pecans; set aside 3/4 cup for topping. Press remaining crumb mixture into a greased 8-in. square baking pan. Bake at 350° for 15 minutes or until edges are lightly browned. Cool on a wire rack. In a mixing bowl, beat cream cheese and sugar. Beat in the pumpkin, eggs, vanilla, cinnamon and allspice. Pour over crust. Sprinkle with reserved crumb mixture. Bake for 30-35 minutes or until golden brown. Cool on a wire rack. Cut into bars. Store in the refrigerator. **Yield:** 16 bars.

Crispy Date Bars

Anna Sheehan, Spokane, Washington

I make these chewy bars around the holidays because they make a nice-size batch for my family. Plus, they keep well in the refrigerator, so I can make them when it's convenient.

  1 cup all-purpose flour
1/2 cup packed brown sugar
1/2 cup cold butter *or* margarine
FILLING:
  1 cup chopped dates
1/2 cup sugar
1/2 cup butter *or* margarine
  1 egg, beaten
  2 cups crisp rice cereal
  1 cup chopped nuts
  1 teaspoon vanilla extract
FROSTING:
  1 package (3 ounces) cream cheese, softened
  2 cups confectioners' sugar
1/2 teaspoon vanilla extract

In a bowl, combine the flour and sugar; cut in butter until crumbly. Press into a greased 9-in. square baking pan. Bake at 375° for 10-12 minutes or until golden brown. Meanwhile, in a heavy saucepan, combine dates, sugar and butter; bring to a boil. Reduce heat; cook and stir for 3 minutes. Add 1/2 cup hot mixture to egg; return all to pan. Bring to a boil. Remove from the heat; stir in cereal, nuts and vanilla. Spread over crust. Cool on a wire rack. In a mixing bowl, combine frosting ingredients; beat until creamy. Frost cooled bars; cut and store in the refrigerator. **Yield:** 2 dozen.

Coconut Graham Cracker Squares

Mrs. Victor Wheeler, Girard, Pennsylvania

These bar cookies travel well and feed a lot of people at potlucks and family reunions. Kids especially like their rich flavor.

- 1 cup butter *or* margarine
- 1 cup sugar
- 1/2 cup milk
- 1 egg, beaten
- 1 cup flaked coconut
- 1 cup chopped walnuts
- 1 cup graham cracker crumbs (about 16 squares)
- 24 whole graham crackers

FROSTING:
- 1/4 cup butter *or* margarine, softened
- 2 cups confectioners' sugar
- 2 tablespoons milk
- 1 teaspoon vanilla extract
- 1/8 teaspoon salt

In a heavy saucepan, melt butter. Stir in sugar, milk and egg. Bring to a boil; cook and stir for 10 minutes. Remove from the heat. Stir in coconut, nuts and cracker crumbs. Line a greased 15-in. x 10-in. x 1-in. baking pan with 12 whole crackers. Spread with the coconut mixture. Top with remaining crackers; press down gently. Cover with plastic wrap and refrigerate for 30 minutes. Meanwhile, in a mixing bowl, combine frosting ingredients; beat until smooth. Break each cracker into four portions; spread with frosting. **Yield:** 4 dozen.

Strawberry Jam Bars

Patricia Olson, Barstow, California

There's a golden crust nicely seasoned with nutmeg, allspice and honey on these sweet bars. The recipe was given to me by an aunt.

- 1/2 cup butter *or* margarine, softened
- 3/4 cup sugar
- 1 egg
- 1 tablespoon honey
- 1-1/4 cups all-purpose flour
- 1/4 teaspoon baking powder
- 1/8 teaspoon ground allspice
- 1/8 teaspoon ground nutmeg
- 2/3 cup strawberry jam
- 1/2 cup chopped walnuts

In a mixing bowl, cream butter and sugar. Beat in egg and honey. Combine the flour, baking powder, all-

spice and nutmeg; gradually add to creamed mixture. Divide the dough in half; spread half into a lightly greased 9-in. square baking pan. Spread with jam. Drop remaining dough by teaspoonfuls over jam. Sprinkle with walnuts. Bake at 350° for 25-30 minutes or until top is golden brown. Cool on a wire rack. Cut into bars. **Yield:** 16 bars.

Dreamy Chocolate Chip Bars

Katharine Fly, Farwell, Texas

This recipe is my children's favorite (and mine!). For even more sweet flavor, they always ask me to dust the bars with confectioners' sugar.

- 1 cup plus 2 tablespoons all-purpose flour, *divided*
- 1 cup quick-cooking oats
- 1-1/2 cups packed brown sugar, *divided*
- 1/2 cup cold butter *or* margarine
- 2 eggs
- 2 teaspoons vanilla extract
- 1-1/2 cups flaked coconut
- 1 cup chopped walnuts
- 1 teaspoon baking powder
- 1/4 teaspoon salt
- 1 cup (6 ounces) semisweet chocolate chips

In a bowl, combine 1 cup flour, oats and 1/2 cup brown sugar; cut in butter until crumbly. Press into a greased 13-in. x 9-in. x 2-in. baking pan. Bake at 375° for 8-10 minutes or until golden brown. Cool on a wire rack. In a mixing bowl, beat eggs, vanilla and remaining brown sugar. Combine the coconut, walnuts, baking powder, salt and remaining flour; gradually add to egg mixture. Stir in chocolate chips. Spread evenly over crust. Bake for 18-20 minutes or until golden brown. Cut into bars while warm. Cool on a wire rack. **Yield:** 4 dozen.

Cranberry Nut Bars

Karen Jarocki, Monte Vista, Colorado

My husband's aunt sent us these bars one Christmas. The fresh cranberry flavor was such a nice change from the usual cookies. I had to have the recipe, and she was gracious enough to provide it.

- 1/2 cup butter *or* margarine, softened
- 3/4 cup sugar
- 3/4 cup packed brown sugar
- 2 eggs
- 1 teaspoon vanilla extract
- 1-1/2 cups all-purpose flour
- 1 teaspoon baking powder

1/2 teaspoon salt
1 cup chopped fresh *or* frozen cranberries
1/2 cup chopped walnuts

In a mixing bowl, cream butter and sugars. Add the eggs, one at a time, beating well after each addition. Beat in vanilla. Combine the flour, baking powder and salt; gradually add to creamed mixture. Stir in cranberries and walnuts. Spread into a greased 13-in. x 9-in. x 2-in. baking pan. Bake at 350° for 20-25 minutes or until golden brown. Cool on a wire rack. Cut into bars. **Yield:** 3 dozen.

Tom Thumb Treats

Virginia Mellinger, Sutherlin, Oregon

This recipe from my mother-in-law dates back to the 1930's. My husband makes them just once a year, at Christmas, but they are worth waiting for!

1 cup all-purpose flour
1/2 cup packed brown sugar
1/2 teaspoon salt
1/2 cup shortening
TOPPING:
2 eggs
1 cup packed brown sugar
1 teaspoon vanilla extract
2 tablespoons all-purpose flour
1/2 teaspoon baking powder
1/4 teaspoon salt
1-1/2 cups flaked coconut
1 cup chopped walnuts

In a bowl, combine flour, brown sugar and salt. Cut in shortening until the mixture resembles coarse crumbs. Press into a greased 13-in. x 9-in. x 2-in. baking pan. Bake at 325° for 12-15 minutes or until golden brown. In a mixing bowl, beat eggs, brown sugar and vanilla until foamy. Combine flour, baking powder and salt; gradually add to the egg mixture. Stir in coconut and nuts. Spread over crust. Bake for 20 minutes or until golden brown. Cool on a wire rack. Cut into bars. **Yield:** 3-1/2 dozen.

Raspberry Almond Bars

Ann Midkiff, Jackson, Michigan

A pan of these thick bars makes a pretty presentation at any gathering. Almond extract is a nice complement to the buttery crust.

2 cups butter *or* margarine, softened
2 cups sugar

2 eggs
1 teaspoon almond extract
5 cups all-purpose flour
1 teaspoon baking powder
1 jar (12 ounces) raspberry jam

In a mixing bowl, cream butter and sugar. Add eggs, one at a time, beating well after each addition. Beat in extract. Combine flour and baking powder; gradually add to the creamed mixture. Press into a greased 13-in. x 9-in. x 2-in. baking pan. With a moistened finger, make diagonal indentations every 2 in. in both directions, about 1/3 in. deep. Fill indentations with jam. Bake at 350° for 40 minutes or until lightly browned. Cool on a wire rack. Cut into bars. **Yield:** about 3 dozen.

Oatmeal Date Bars

Elnora Hamel, Greenville, Illinois

I've been making these bars for almost 50 years. I remember my dad saying they were the best he ever tasted. Use your food processor to easily grind the oats.

2 cups quick-cooking oats
3/4 cup shortening
1/2 cup sugar
2 cups all-purpose flour
1 teaspoon baking soda
1/2 teaspoon salt
1/2 cup buttermilk
FILLING:
3 cups chopped dates (about 1 pound)
1 cup sugar
1 cup water
1 to 2 tablespoons lemon juice, optional
GLAZE:
1-1/2 cups confectioners' sugar
1/8 teaspoon salt
1 teaspoon vanilla extract
3 tablespoons milk

In a blender or food processor, process oats until finely ground; set aside. In a mixing bowl, cream shortening and sugar. Combine oats, flour, baking soda and salt; add to creamed mixture alternately with buttermilk. Divide in half. On a lightly floured surface, roll half of dough to fit a greased 13-in. x 9-in. x 2-in. baking pan; set aside. In a saucepan, combine dates, sugar, water and lemon juice if desired; bring to a boil, stirring constantly. Cook and stir until thickened, about 6 minutes. Cool slightly, about 10 minutes. Spread over crust. Roll remaining dough to fit pan; place over filling and seal edges. Bake at 400° for 15-20 minutes or until crust is golden brown. Combine glaze ingredients; spread over bars while warm. Cool on a wire rack before cutting. **Yield:** 3 dozen.

Refrigerator Favorites

Double Butterscotch Cookies

Beverly Duncan, Big Prairie, Ohio

(Pictured at left)

This is a very old recipe that's been in the family for generations. Sometimes I'll omit the toffee bits and add miniature chocolate chips or coconut instead.

    1/2 cup butter *or* margarine, softened
    1/2 cup shortening
      4 cups packed brown sugar
      4 eggs
      1 tablespoon vanilla extract
      6 cups all-purpose flour
      1 tablespoon baking soda
      1 tablespoon cream of tartar
      1 teaspoon salt
      1 package English toffee bits (10 ounces) *or*
        almond brickle chips (7-1/2 ounces)
      1 cup finely chopped pecans

In a mixing bowl, cream the butter, shortening and brown sugar. Add eggs, one at a time, beating well after each addition. Beat in vanilla. Combine flour, baking soda, cream of tartar and salt; gradually add to the creamed mixture. Stir in toffee bits and pecans. Shape into three 14-in. rolls; wrap each in plastic wrap. Refrigerate for 4 hours or until firm. Unwrap and cut into 1/2-in. slices. Place 2 in. apart on greased baking sheets. Bake at 375° for 9-11 minutes or until lightly browned. Cool for 1-2 minutes before removing to wire racks to cool completely. **Yield:** about 7 dozen.

Cappuccino Flats

Jacqueline Cline, Drummond, Wisconsin

(Pictured at left)

These coffee-flavored cookies are so delicious most people can't believe they're made in my own kitchen instead of a gourmet bakery!

    1/2 cup butter *or* margarine, softened
    1/2 cup shortening

> **SAVORY SLICES.** Pictured at left, clockwise from upper left: Double Butterscotch Cookies, Cappuccino Flats and Lemon Poppy Seed Slices (all recipes on this page).

    1/2 cup sugar
    1/2 cup packed brown sugar
      1 tablespoon instant coffee granules
      1 teaspoon warm water
      1 egg
      2 squares (1 ounce *each*) unsweetened
        chocolate, melted and cooled
      2 cups all-purpose flour
      1 teaspoon ground cinnamon
    1/4 teaspoon salt
    1-1/2 cups semisweet chocolate chips
      3 tablespoons shortening

In a mixing bowl, cream butter, shortening and sugars. Dissolve coffee in water; add to creamed mixture with egg and melted chocolate. Mix well. Combine flour, cinnamon and salt; gradually add to creamed mixture (dough will be sticky). Shape into two 6-1/2-in. rolls; wrap each in plastic wrap. Refrigerate for 4 hours or until firm. Unwrap and cut into 1/4-in. slices. Place 2 in. apart on ungreased baking sheets. Bake at 350° for 10-12 minutes or until firm. Remove to wire racks to cool. In a small saucepan over low heat, melt chocolate chips and shortening. Dip each cookie halfway; shake off excess. Place on waxed paper to harden. **Yield:** about 4-1/2 dozen.

Lemon Poppy Seed Slices

Pauline Piraino, Bay Shore, New York

(Pictured at left)

My mom taught me to bake, and I use lots of recipes from her abundant collection, including this one.

    3/4 cup butter (no substitutes), softened
      1 cup sugar
      1 egg
      1 tablespoon milk
      2 teaspoons finely grated lemon peel
    1/2 teaspoon vanilla extract
    1/2 teaspoon lemon extract, optional
    2-1/2 cups all-purpose flour
    1/4 cup poppy seeds

In a mixing bowl, cream butter and sugar. Beat in egg, milk, lemon peel and extracts. Add flour and poppy seeds; mix well. Shape into two 8-in. rolls; wrap each in plastic wrap. Refrigerate for 3 hours or until firm. Unwrap and cut into 1/4-in. slices. Place 2 in. apart on ungreased baking sheets. Bake at 350° for 10-12 minutes or until edges are golden. Cool for 2 minutes before removing to wire racks to cool completely. **Yield:** 5-1/2 dozen.

Date Nut Icebox Cookies

Gladys Maurer, Laramie, Wyoming

A dear friend shared this recipe with me many years ago. They've become a much-requested treat at my house, so it's a good thing the recipe yields a big batch!

> 1 cup butter *or* margarine, softened
> 1 cup shortening
> 2-1/2 cups sugar
> 2 eggs
> 1-1/2 teaspoons vanilla extract
> 1 tablespoon light corn syrup
> 5 cups all-purpose flour
> 1 teaspoon salt
> 1 teaspoon baking soda
> 1 cup finely chopped walnuts
> 1 cup finely chopped dates

In a mixing bowl, cream the butter, shortening and sugar. Add eggs, one at a time, beating well after each addition. Beat in vanilla and corn syrup. Combine flour, salt and baking soda; gradually add to the creamed mixture. Stir in walnuts and dates. Shape into four 6-in. rolls; wrap each in plastic wrap. Refrigerate overnight. Unwrap and cut into 1/4-in. slices. Place 2-1/2 in. apart on ungreased baking sheets. Bake at 375° for 10-12 minutes or until lightly browned. Cool for 2-3 minutes before removing to wire racks to cool completely. **Yield:** about 8 dozen.

Mom's Coconut Cookies

Shirley Secrest, Mattoon, Illinois

Mom worked hard to keep us fed during the Depression, and there was never a day we went hungry. These cookies could always be found in the cookie jar.

> 1/2 cup butter *or* margarine, softened
> 1 cup sugar
> 1/4 cup packed brown sugar
> 1 egg
> 1-1/2 teaspoons vanilla extract
> 2 cups all-purpose flour
> 1-1/2 teaspoons baking powder
> 1/8 teaspoon salt
> 1 cup flaked coconut

In a mixing bowl, cream butter and sugars. Beat in egg and vanilla. Combine the flour, baking powder and salt; gradually add to the creamed mixture. Stir in coconut. Shape into two 3-1/2-in. rolls; wrap each in plastic wrap. Refrigerate for 2 hours or until firm. Unwrap and cut into 1/8-in. slices. Place 2 in. apart on ungreased baking sheets. Bake at 425° for

5-7 minutes or until lightly browned. Remove to wire racks to cool. **Yield:** 5 dozen.

Butterscotch Bonanza Cookies

Dorothy Hankey, Waukesha, Wisconsin

These cookies store well for about 2 weeks in an airtight container. So when you have some time to spare, make a batch and enjoy them for days to come.

> 1 cup butter *or* margarine, softened
> 3 cups packed brown sugar
> 4 eggs, *separated*
> 5-1/2 cups all-purpose flour
> 1 teaspoon baking soda
> 1 teaspoon cream of tartar
> 1 cup chopped almonds

In a mixing bowl, cream butter and brown sugar. Add egg yolks, one at a time, beating well after each addition. Combine flour, baking soda and cream of tartar; gradually add to the creamed mixture. Stir in almonds. In small mixing bowl, beat egg whites until stiff peaks form; fold into dough. Shape into four 9-in. rolls; wrap each in plastic wrap. Refrigerate overnight. Unwrap and cut into 1/8- to 1/4-in. slices. Place 1 in. apart on greased baking sheets. Bake at 350° for 10-12 minutes or until edges are golden brown. Remove to wire racks to cool. **Yield:** about 12 dozen.

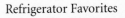

Ginger Nut Crisps

Dellene Love, Hood River, Oregon

The only problem with these cookies is that it's hard to eat just one! I came up with this recipe when my mother shared a large supply of ginger. We love these spice cookies.

> 1 cup butter *or* margarine, softened
> 1 cup sugar
> 3/4 cup honey
> 3 cups all-purpose flour
> 1 cup whole wheat flour
> 1 tablespoon ground cinnamon
> 1 tablespoon ground cloves
> 2 to 3 teaspoons ground ginger
> 1-1/2 teaspoons baking soda
> 1 teaspoon salt
> 1-1/2 cups finely chopped pecans *or* almonds

In a mixing bowl, cream butter and sugar. Beat in honey. Combine the flours, cinnamon, cloves, ginger, baking soda and salt; gradually add to the creamed mixture. Stir in nuts. Shape into two 11-in. rolls; wrap each in plastic wrap. Refrigerate for 3 hours or until firm. Unwrap and cut into 1/4-in. slices. Place 2 in. apart on ungreased baking sheets. Bake at 375° for 8-11 minutes or until firm. Remove to wire racks to cool. **Yield:** 6 dozen.

Lemon Refrigerator Cookies

Dessa Black, Dallas, Texas

This recipe brings back warm memories of watching my mom bake when I was a girl. To this day, the holidays wouldn't be the same without these cookies.

> 1/2 cup butter *or* margarine, softened
> 1/2 cup sugar
> 1/2 cup packed brown sugar
> 1 egg
> 1 teaspoon vanilla extract
> 1 teaspoon lemon extract
> 1-3/4 cups all-purpose flour
> 1/2 teaspoon baking soda
> 1/4 teaspoon salt
> 1/2 cup finely chopped pecans

In a mixing bowl, cream butter and sugars. Beat in the egg and extracts. Combine flour, baking soda and salt; gradually add to the creamed mixture. Stir in pecans. Shape into two 9-in. rolls; wrap each in plastic wrap. Refrigerate for 2 hours or until firm. Unwrap and cut into 1/8-in. slices. Place 1 in. apart on ungreased baking sheets. Bake at 250° for 21-22 minutes or until edges are golden brown. Remove to wire racks to cool. **Yield:** about 8 dozen. **Editor's Note:** The oven temperature is correct as printed.

Buttermilk Spice Crisps

Marla Mason, Cedar Rapids, Iowa

These cookies were a Christmas tradition for one of the families in my childhood church. I looked forward to caroling at their house because we were rewarded with one of these tasty morsels!

> 1 cup butter *or* margarine, softened
> 2 cups sugar
> 1 egg
> 1/3 cup buttermilk
> 4-2/3 cups all-purpose flour
> 2 teaspoons baking soda
> 2 teaspoons ground cinnamon
> 1 teaspoon *each* ground allspice, cloves and nutmeg

In a mixing bowl, cream butter and sugar. Beat in egg and buttermilk. Combine flour, baking soda, cinnamon, allspice, cloves and nutmeg; gradually add to

the creamed mixture. Shape into two 9-in. rolls; wrap each in plastic wrap. Refrigerate for 4 hours or until firm. Unwrap and cut into 1/4-in. slices. Place 2 in. apart on ungreased baking sheets. Bake at 350° for 10-12 minutes or until golden brown. Remove to wire racks to cool. **Yield:** 6 dozen.

Sugar Cookie Slices

Lonna Peterman, New Port Richey, Florida

I was fortunate to inherit this recipe from my husband's great-aunt. They slice nicely and are easier to make than traditional cutout sugar cookies.

> 1-1/2 cups butter *or* margarine, softened
> 1-1/2 cups sugar
> 1/2 teaspoon vanilla extract
> 3 cups all-purpose flour
> 1 teaspoon baking soda
> 1/2 teaspoon salt

In a mixing bowl, cream butter and sugar. Beat in vanilla. Combine flour, baking soda and salt; gradually add to the creamed mixture. Shape into two 8-in. rolls; wrap each in plastic wrap. Refrigerate for 4 hours or until firm. Unwrap and cut into 1/4-in. slices. Place 2 in. apart on ungreased baking sheets. Bake at 350° for 12-14 minutes or until set (do not brown). Remove to wire racks to cool. **Yield:** 5 dozen.

Pecan Rounds

Clara Avilla, San Martin, California

I developed this recipe when a friend shared her pecan crop with me. These cookies are always on my family's "must make" list.

> 1 cup butter (no substitutes), softened
> 1-1/2 cups confectioners' sugar, *divided*
> 1 teaspoon vanilla extract
> 2-1/4 cups all-purpose flour
> 3/4 cup finely ground pecans, toasted
> 1/2 teaspoon salt
> 1 tablespoon ground cinnamon

In a mixing bowl, cream the butter and 1/2 cup sugar. Beat in vanilla. Combine flour, pecans and salt; gradually add to the creamed mixture. Shape into two 8-in. rolls; wrap each in plastic wrap. Refrigerate for 2 hours or until firm. Unwrap and cut into 1/4-in. slices. Place 1-1/2 in. apart on ungreased baking sheets. Bake at 375° for 8-10 minutes or until edges are lightly browned. Meanwhile, combine cinnamon and remaining sugar. Roll warm cookies in cinnamon-sugar. Cool on wire racks. **Yield:** 6-1/2 dozen.

Toffee Cranberry Crisps

Ann Quaerna, Lake Geneva, Wisconsin

I've had more friends request this recipe than any other cookie recipe I have. The combination of cranberries, chocolate chips and toffee bits is wonderful.

> 1 cup butter (no substitutes), softened
> 3/4 cup sugar
> 3/4 cup packed brown sugar
> 1 egg
> 1 teaspoon vanilla extract
> 1-1/2 cups all-purpose flour
> 1-1/2 cups quick-cooking oats
> 1 teaspoon baking soda
> 1/4 teaspoon salt
> 1 cup dried cranberries
> 1 cup miniature semisweet chocolate chips
> 1 cup English toffee bits *or* almond brickle chips

In a mixing bowl, cream butter and sugars. Beat in egg and vanilla. Combine flour, oats, baking soda and salt; gradually add to creamed mixture. Stir in cranberries, chocolate chips and toffee bits. Shape into three 12-in. rolls; wrap each in plastic wrap. Refrigerate for 2 hours or until firm. Unwrap and cut into 1/2-in. slices. Place 2 in. apart on ungreased baking sheets. Bake at 350° for 8-10 minutes or until golden brown. Remove to wire racks to cool. **Yield:** 5-1/2 dozen.

Rainbow Swirls

Gail Russler, Lander, Wyoming

The students in my home economics class enjoy choosing and mixing in the food coloring for these cookies.

> 1/2 cup butter *or* margarine, softened
> 1/2 cup shortening
> 1 cup sugar
> 1 egg
> 1 teaspoon vanilla extract
> 2 cups all-purpose flour
> 1/2 teaspoon baking powder
> Green and red liquid food coloring

In a mixing bowl, cream butter, shortening and sugar. Beat in egg and vanilla. Combine flour and baking powder; gradually add to creamed mixture. Divide dough into three portions. Tint one portion pink and one green. Leave one portion plain. Refrigerate for 30 minutes or until easy to handle. Shape each portion into a 15-in. roll. Place all three rolls on a large piece of plastic wrap. Wrap tightly; roll gently until rolls form one log. Refrigerate overnight. Unwrap and

cut into 1/4-in. slices. Place 2 in. apart on ungreased baking sheets. Bake at 375° for 10-12 minutes or until the edges are lightly browned. Remove to wire racks to cool. **Yield:** about 4 dozen.

Mint Wafers

Barrie Citrowske, Canby, Minnesota

I enjoy nibbling on these cookies with a cup of tea or coffee for a midday treat. For even more mint flavor, use mint chocolate chips instead of semisweet.

> 1 cup butter *or* margarine, softened
> 3/4 cup sugar
> 1 egg
> 1/4 teaspoon peppermint extract
> 2-1/4 cups all-purpose flour
> 1/2 teaspoon salt
> 1 cup (6 ounces) semisweet chocolate chips
> 4 teaspoons shortening

In a mixing bowl, cream butter and sugar. Beat in egg and extract. Combine flour and salt; gradually add to the creamed mixture. Shape into two 8-in. rolls; wrap each in plastic wrap. Refrigerate for 3 hours or until firm. Unwrap and cut into 1/4-in. slices. Place 1 in. apart on ungreased baking sheets. Bake at 350° for 9-10 minutes or until the edges begin to brown. Remove to wire racks to cool. In a double boiler or microwave, melt chocolate and shortening; stir until smooth. Spread or drizzle over cookies. **Yield:** about 6 dozen.

Cream Cheese-Filled Cookies

Ruth Glick, New Holland, Pennsylvania

My aunt baked these cookies as part of my wedding day dinner. Everyone was impressed with their eye-catching appeal and rich flavor.

> 1/3 cup butter *or* margarine, softened
> 1/3 cup shortening
> 3/4 cup sugar
> 1 egg
> 1 teaspoon vanilla extract
> 1-3/4 cups all-purpose flour
> 1 teaspoon baking powder
> 1/2 teaspoon salt
> FILLING:
> 2 packages (3 ounces *each*) cream cheese, softened
> 1-1/2 cups confectioners' sugar
> 2 tablespoons all-purpose flour
> 1 teaspoon vanilla extract
> 1 drop yellow food coloring, optional

TOPPING:
   3/4 cup semisweet chocolate chips
   3 tablespoons butter *or* margarine

In a mixing bowl, cream butter, shortening and sugar. Beat in egg and vanilla. Combine flour, baking powder and salt; gradually add to the creamed mixture. Shape into two 12-in. rolls; wrap each in plastic wrap. Refrigerate for 4 hours or overnight. Unwrap and cut into 1-in. slices. Place 1 in. apart on greased baking sheets. Bake at 375° for 10-12 minutes or until lightly browned. Remove to wire racks to cool. Combine filling ingredients in a mixing bowl; mix well. Place 2 teaspoonfuls in the center of each cookie. Let stand until set. In a small saucepan over low heat, melt chocolate chips and butter; stir until smooth. Drizzle over cookies. Store in the refrigerator. **Yield:** about 2-1/2 dozen.

Pecan Icebox Cookies

Angi Rogman, Seattle, Washington

My best friend's grandmother frequently makes these old-fashioned cookies and was kind enough to pass the treasured family recipe on to me.

   1 cup butter *or* margarine, softened
   1 cup sugar
   1 cup packed brown sugar
   3 eggs
   4 cups all-purpose flour
   2 teaspoons baking powder
   1 teaspoon baking soda
   1 teaspoon ground cinnamon
   1/2 teaspoon salt
   1 cup chopped pecans

In a mixing bowl, cream butter and sugars. Add the eggs, one at a time, beating well after each addition. Combine flour, baking powder, baking soda, cinnamon and salt; gradually add to the creamed mixture. Stir in pecans. Shape into four 6-1/2-in. rolls; wrap each in plastic wrap. Refrigerate overnight. Unwrap and cut into 1/8-in. slices. Place 1 in. apart on ungreased baking sheets. Bake at 375° for 7-10 minutes or until lightly browned. Remove to wire racks to cool. **Yield:** about 9 dozen.

Caramel Swirls

Jan Smith, Star, Texas

In my opinion, cookies are the best dessert to make… and to eat! With a crisp outside and chewy caramel filling, these are likely one of my very favorites.

   1 cup butter (no substitutes), softened
   4 ounces cream cheese, softened
   1 cup packed brown sugar
   1 egg yolk
   1 teaspoon maple flavoring
2-3/4 cups all-purpose flour
FILLING:
   30 caramels
   2 packages (3 ounces *each*) cream cheese, softened

In a mixing bowl, cream butter, cream cheese and brown sugar. Add egg yolk and maple flavoring; mix well. Gradually add flour. Refrigerate for 2 hours or until easy to handle. Meanwhile, in a saucepan or microwave, melt caramels. Stir in cream cheese until blended; set aside. Divide dough in half. Roll each portion between waxed paper to 1/4-in. thickness. Spread caramel mixture over dough to within 1/2 in. of edges. Roll up tightly, jelly-roll style, starting with a long side. Wrap each roll in plastic wrap. Refrigerate for 4 hours or until firm. Unwrap and cut into 1/4-in. slices. Place 1 in. apart on greased baking sheets. Bake at 350° for 12-14 minutes or until golden brown. Remove to wire racks to cool. **Yield:** 6-1/2 dozen.

Chocolate Pinwheels

Denise Hufford, Midland, Michigan

This recipe evolved from several different recipes that I combined into one. I've never received so many compliments on my baking!

   1 cup butter (no substitutes), softened
   2 cups sugar
   1/2 cup packed brown sugar
   2 eggs
   3 teaspoons vanilla extract
3-3/4 cups all-purpose flour
   2 teaspoons baking powder
   1/8 teaspoon salt
   1/4 cup baking cocoa

In a mixing bowl, cream butter and sugars. Add the eggs, one at a time, beating well after each. Beat in vanilla. Combine flour, baking powder and salt; gradually add to the creamed mixture. Divide dough in half; add cocoa to one portion. Divide each portion in half. On a baking sheet, roll out each portion between waxed paper into a 12-in. x 10-in. rectangle. Refrigerate for 30 minutes. Remove waxed paper. Place one chocolate rectangle over a plain rectangle. Roll up tightly, jelly-roll style, starting with a long side; wrap in plastic wrap. Repeat with remaining dough. Refrigerate for 2 hours or until firm. Unwrap and cut into 1/4-in. slices. Place 2 in. apart on lightly greased baking sheets. Bake at 350° for 10-12 minutes or until set. Remove to wire racks to cool. **Yield:** 6 dozen.

Sandwich Cookies

Caramel Creams

Barbara Youngers, Kingman, Kansas

(Pictured at left)

These cookies are delicious plain, but I like to make them into sandwich cookies with the brown butter filling. In a pinch, you can use a can of frosting.

- 1 cup butter (no substitutes), softened
- 2/3 cup packed brown sugar
- 2 egg yolks
- 1/2 teaspoon vanilla extract
- 2-1/2 cups all-purpose flour
- 1/3 cup finely chopped pecans
- 1/4 teaspoon salt

FILLING:
- 2 tablespoons plus 1-1/2 teaspoons butter (no substitutes)
- 1-1/2 cups confectioners' sugar
- 1/2 teaspoon vanilla extract
- 2 to 3 tablespoons whipping cream

In a mixing bowl, cream butter and brown sugar. Beat in egg yolks and vanilla. Combine flour, pecans and salt; gradually add to the creamed mixture. Shape into two 10-in. rolls; wrap each in plastic wrap. Refrigerate for 1-2 hours. Unwrap and cut into 1/4-in. slices. Place 2 in. apart on ungreased baking sheets. Bake at 350° for 11-13 minutes or until golden brown. Remove to wire racks to cool. For filling, heat butter in a saucepan over medium heat until golden brown. Remove from the heat; add confectioners' sugar, vanilla and enough cream to achieve spreading consistency. Spread on the bottom of half of the cookies; top with remaining cookies. **Yield:** about 3 dozen.

Cream-Filled Chocolate Cookies

Maxine Finn, Emmetsburg, Iowa

(Pictured at left)

I've been making these cookies for years. My children and grandchildren gobble them up.

> **FILLED FAVORITES.** Pictured at left, top to bottom: Caramel Creams, Cream-Filled Chocolate Cookies (recipes on this page) and Almond Jelly Cookies (recipe on page 98).

- 1 cup butter (no substitutes), softened
- 2 cups sugar
- 2 eggs
- 1 teaspoon vanilla extract
- 3 cups all-purpose flour
- 2/3 cup baking cocoa
- 1 teaspoon baking soda
- 1 teaspoon salt
- 1/2 cup milk

FILLING:
- 1/2 cup butter *or* margarine, softened
- 1-1/2 cups confectioners' sugar
- 1 cup marshmallow creme
- 1 teaspoon vanilla extract

In a mixing bowl, cream butter and sugar. Add eggs, one at a time, beating well after each addition. Beat in vanilla. Combine the flour, cocoa, baking soda and salt; add to creamed mixture alternately with milk. Refrigerate for at least 2 hours. Drop by rounded teaspoonfuls 2 in. apart onto greased baking sheets. Bake at 375° for 10-12 minutes or until edges are set. Remove to wire racks to cool. Combine filling ingredients in a small mixing bowl; beat until smooth. Spread on the bottom of half of the cookies; top with remaining cookies. Store in the refrigerator. **Yield:** about 4-1/2 dozen.

Maple Sandwich Cookies

Barbara Scacchi, Limestone, New York

Mom loves maple flavoring, so I created this recipe just for her. But the whole family loves these tasty cookies.

- 1 cup butter *or* margarine, softened
- 3/4 cup packed brown sugar
- 1 egg yolk
- 2 cups all-purpose flour
- Sugar

FILLING:
- 1-1/4 cups confectioners' sugar
- 2 tablespoons milk
- 2 tablespoons butter *or* margarine, softened
- 1/2 teaspoon maple flavoring

In a mixing bowl, cream butter and brown sugar. Beat in the egg yolk and flour; mix well. Shape into 1-in. balls. Dip the tops in sugar. Place sugar side up 2 in. apart on ungreased baking sheets. Flatten with a fork. Bake at 325° for 10-12 minutes or until golden brown. Remove to wire racks to cool. Combine filling ingredients in a small mixing bowl; beat until smooth. Spread on the bottom of half of the cookies; top with remaining cookies. **Yield:** about 3 dozen.

Oatmeal Sandwich Cremes

Lesley Mansfield, Monroe, North Carolina

These hearty cookies appeal to all palates whenever I take them to a family get-together or church bake sale. They're worth the little extra effort!

     3/4 cup shortening
       1 cup sugar
       1 cup packed brown sugar
       1 egg
     1/4 cup water
       1 teaspoon vanilla extract
1-1/2 cups self-rising flour*
       1 teaspoon baking soda
       1 teaspoon ground cinnamon
       3 cups quick-cooking oats
     3/4 cup raisins
FILLING:
     1/2 cup butter *or* margarine, softened
     1/2 cup shortening
3-3/4 cups confectioners' sugar
       2 tablespoons milk
       1 teaspoon vanilla extract
Dash salt

In a mixing bowl, cream shortening and sugars. Beat in egg, water and vanilla. Combine flour, baking soda and cinnamon; gradually add to the creamed mixture. Stir in oats and raisins. Drop by tablespoonfuls 3 in. apart onto ungreased baking sheets. Flatten with a glass. Bake at 325° for 13-14 minutes or until lightly browned. Remove to wire racks to cool. Combine filling ingredients in a mixing bowl; beat until smooth. Spread on the bottom of half of the cookies; top with remaining cookies. **Yield:** 3 dozen.
*Editor's Note: As a substitute for 1 cup self-rising flour, place 1-1/2 teaspoons baking powder and 1/2 teaspoon salt in a measuring cup; add all-purpose flour to measure 1 cup. For 1/2 cup, place 3/4 teaspoon baking powder and 1/4 teaspoon salt in a 1/2-cup measuring cup; add all-purpose flour to measure 1/2 cup.

Raspberry Coconut Cookies

June Brown, Veneta, Oregon

My mother gave me the recipe for these rich buttery cookies. Raspberry preserves and a cream filling make them doubly delicious.

     3/4 cup butter *or* margarine, softened
     1/2 cup sugar
       1 egg
       1 teaspoon vanilla extract
       2 cups all-purpose flour
     1/2 cup flaked coconut
1-1/2 teaspoons baking powder
     1/4 teaspoon salt
FILLING:
     1/4 cup butter *or* margarine, softened
     3/4 cup confectioners' sugar
       2 teaspoons milk
     1/2 teaspoon vanilla extract
     1/2 cup raspberry preserves

In a mixing bowl, cream butter and sugar. Beat in egg and vanilla. Combine flour, coconut, baking powder and salt; gradually add to the creamed mixture. Shape into 1-in. balls. Place 1-1/2 in. apart on ungreased baking sheets; flatten with a glass dipped in flour. Bake at 350° for 12-14 minutes or until edges are very light brown. Cool on wire racks. In a mixing bowl, combine the first four filling ingredients; beat until smooth. Place 1/2 teaspoon preserves and a scant teaspoon of filling on the bottom of half of the cookies; top with remaining cookies. **Yield:** 2-1/2 dozen.

Cranberry Lemon Sandwiches

Patricia Michalski, Oswego, New York

I bake cookies all year long, so my friends and family call me the "Cookie Lady"! Whenever I bake these for Christmas, I make three batches…one to keep at home for my husband and two to give as gifts.

       1 cup butter *or* margarine, softened
       1 cup shortening
       1 cup sugar
       1 cup confectioners' sugar
       2 eggs
       2 teaspoons vanilla extract
       4 cups all-purpose flour
       1 teaspoon cream of tartar
       1 teaspoon grated lemon peel
     1/2 teaspoon salt
     3/4 cup dried cranberries
FILLING:
     2/3 cup butter *or* margarine, softened
2-3/4 cups confectioners' sugar
     1/4 cup milk
1-1/4 teaspoons grated lemon peel

In a mixing bowl, cream butter, shortening and sugars. Add eggs, one at a time, beating well after each addition. Beat in vanilla. Combine flour, cream of tartar, lemon peel and salt; gradually add to the creamed mixture. Stir in cranberries. Cover and refrigerate for 2 hours or until easy to handle. Roll into 1-in. balls. Place 2 in. apart on ungreased baking sheets. Flatten with a glass dipped in sugar. Bake at 350° for 12-14 minutes or until edges are lightly browned. Remove to wire racks to cool. Combine filling ingredients in a mixing bowl; beat until smooth. Spread on the bottom of half of the cookies; top with remaining cookies. **Yield:** about 4-1/2 dozen.

Buttercups

Alice Le Duc, Cedarburg, Wisconsin

These cookies began as simple Christmas cutouts. One day I decided to make them with a brown butter filling. Sometimes I'll fill the centers with melted chocolate.

  1 cup butter (no substitutes), softened
1-1/2 cups confectioners' sugar
  1 egg
  1 teaspoon vanilla extract
2-1/2 cups all-purpose flour
FILLING:
  1/4 cup butter (no substitutes)
1-1/2 cups confectioners' sugar
  3/4 teaspoon vanilla extract
  5 tablespoons water
  1/4 cup raspberry preserves *or* fruit preserves of your choice

In a mixing bowl, cream butter and sugar. Beat in egg and vanilla. Gradually add flour. Divide dough in half; wrap each portion in plastic wrap. Refrigerate for 2 hours or until easy to handle; unwrap. On a lightly floured surface, roll out each portion of dough to 1/8-in. thickness. Cut with a 2-1/2-in. scalloped cookie cutter dipped in flour. Cut a 1-in. hole in the center of half of the cookies with a bottle cap. Place 2 in. apart on ungreased baking sheets. Bake at 375° for 8-10 minutes or until lightly browned. Remove to wire racks to cool. In a saucepan, heat butter over medium heat until golden brown. Remove from the heat; gradually add sugar, vanilla and enough water to achieve a spreading consistency. Spread on the bottom of the solid cookies; place cookies with cutout centers over filling so the scalloped edges alternate. Place 1/2 teaspoon preserves in center of each. **Yield:** 3 dozen.

Chocolate Almond Cookies

Kathryn Werner, Peterborough, Ontario

Special occasions around our house have always been indicated by these chocolate-dipped, jam-filled cookies. They not only look appealing, they taste terrific, too.

  1/2 cup butter *or* margarine, softened
  6 tablespoons sugar

1-1/2 teaspoons vanilla extract
  1 cup all-purpose flour
  1 cup finely chopped blanched almonds
  1/4 to 1/2 cup raspberry jam *or* jam of your choice
  3 squares (1 ounce *each*) semisweet chocolate, melted

In a mixing bowl, cream butter, sugar and vanilla. Combine flour and almonds; gradually add to the creamed mixture. Shape into one 12-in. roll; wrap in plastic wrap. Refrigerate for 4 hours or until firm. Unwrap; cut into 1/4-in. slices. Place 2 in. apart on ungreased baking sheets. Bake at 350° for 8-10 minutes or until lightly browned. Remove to wire racks to cool. Spread 1 teaspoon jam on the bottom of half of the cookies; top with remaining cookies. Dip cookies halfway into melted chocolate; shake off excess. Place on waxed paper-lined baking sheets to harden. **Yield:** 2 dozen.

Toffee Sandwich Cookies

April McDavid, Centerburg, Ohio

My brother's quest to find a filled toffee cookie inspired me to spend hours in the kitchen coming up with a winning combination. Of the 14 kinds of cookies I bake each Christmas, these are the first to disappear.

  1 cup butter *or* margarine, softened
  1 cup packed brown sugar
  1/2 cup sugar
  2 eggs
  2 teaspoons vanilla extract
2-1/2 cups all-purpose flour
  1/2 teaspoon baking soda
  1/4 teaspoon salt
  1 cup English toffee bits *or* almond brickle chips
FILLING:
  2/3 cup butter *or* margarine, softened
  4 cups confectioners' sugar
  1 teaspoon vanilla extract
  3 to 5 tablespoons half-and-half cream *or* milk

In a mixing bowl, cream butter and sugars. Add eggs, one at a time, beating well after each addition. Beat in vanilla. Combine flour, baking soda and salt; gradually add to the creamed mixture. Stir in toffee bits (dough will be stiff). Drop by rounded teaspoonfuls 2 in. apart onto ungreased baking sheets. Bake at 350° for 10 minutes or until firm (do not brown). In a mixing bowl, combine butter, sugar, vanilla and enough cream to achieve spreading consistency. Spread on the bottom of half of the cookies; top with remaining cookies. **Yield:** 4 dozen.

Bake Sale Bonanza

Chocolate Chip Cookie Pops

Silretta Graves, Park Forest, Illinois

(Pictured at left)

My family prefers milk chocolate to dark or semisweet chocolate, so I created this recipe. Baking the pops on a stick makes them fun, but the cookies are just as delicious by themselves.

     2 cups butter *or* margarine, softened
1-1/2 cups sugar
1-1/2 cups packed brown sugar
     3 eggs
     1 tablespoon vanilla extract
4-3/4 cups all-purpose flour
1-1/2 teaspoons baking soda
     1 teaspoon salt
     3 cups milk chocolate chips
     2 cups chopped pecans
    12 dozen wooden craft *or* Popsicle sticks, optional

In a large mixing bowl, cream the butter and sugars. Add eggs, one at a time, beating well after each addition. Beat in vanilla. Combine flour, baking soda and salt; gradually add to creamed mixture. Transfer to a larger bowl if necessary. Stir in chips and pecans. Drop by rounded teaspoonfuls 3 in. apart onto ungreased baking sheets. Insert a wooden stick into each cookie if desired. Bake at 375° for 10-12 minutes or until lightly browned. Cool for 1-2 minutes before removing to wire racks. **Yield:** about 12 dozen.

Peanut Butter Jumbos

Deborah Huffer, Staunton, Virginia

(Pictured at left)

Oats, peanut butter and chocolate make these soft, chewy cookies hearty and nutritious. My whole family agrees this recipe is a real winner.

1-1/2 cups peanut butter
  1/2 cup butter *or* margarine, softened

> **POTLUCK PLEASERS.** Pictured at left, top to bottom: Chocolate Chip Cookie Pops, Peanut Butter Jumbos and Double Chocolate Sprinkle Cookies (all recipes on this page).

     1 cup sugar
     1 cup packed brown sugar
     3 eggs
     1 teaspoon vanilla extract
4-1/2 cups quick-cooking oats
     2 teaspoons baking soda
     1 cup miniature semisweet chocolate chips
     1 cup miniature M&M's

In a large mixing bowl, cream peanut butter, butter and sugars. Add eggs, one at a time, beating well after each addition. Beat in vanilla. Combine oats and baking soda; gradually add to creamed mixture. Stir in chips and M&M's. Drop by heaping tablespoonfuls 2 in. apart onto ungreased baking sheets. Bake at 350° for 12-14 minutes or until edges are browned. Remove to wire racks to cool. **Yield:** 9 dozen. **Editor's Note:** This recipe does not contain flour.

Double Chocolate Sprinkle Cookies

Barb Meinholz, South Milwaukee, Wisconsin

(Pictured at left)

 Chock-full of chocolate chips and sprinkles, these chewy cookies never last long around our house. They're simply outstanding.

     2 cups butter *or* margarine, softened
     2 cups sugar
     2 cups packed brown sugar
     4 eggs
     2 teaspoons vanilla extract
     5 cups old-fashioned oats
     4 cups all-purpose flour
     2 teaspoons baking soda
     2 teaspoons baking powder
     1 teaspoon salt
     4 cups (24 ounces) semisweet chocolate chips
     3 cups chopped walnuts
     2 cups chocolate sprinkles

In a large mixing bowl, cream the butter and sugars. Add eggs, one at a time, beating well after each addition. Beat in vanilla. Place the oats in a blender or food processor; cover and process until finely ground. Combine oats, flour, baking soda, baking powder and salt; gradually add to creamed mixture. Transfer to a larger bowl if necessary. Stir in chocolate chips, walnuts and sprinkles. Roll into 1-1/2-in. balls. Place 2 in. apart on ungreased baking sheets. Flatten with a glass. Bake at 350° for 12-14 minutes or until golden brown. Remove to wire racks to cool. **Yield:** about 9 dozen.

Tried 'n' True Peanut Butter Cookies

Emma Lee Granger, La Pine, Oregon

When I want to offer friends and family a tried-and-true cookie, this is the recipe I turn to. Use either creamy or crunchy peanut butter with delicious results.

- 4 cups butter-flavored shortening
- 4 cups peanut butter
- 3 cups sugar
- 3 cups packed brown sugar
- 8 eggs
- 4 teaspoons vanilla extract
- 2 teaspoons water
- 9 cups all-purpose flour
- 4 teaspoons baking soda
- 4 teaspoon salt

In a large mixing bowl, cream shortening, peanut butter and sugars. Add eggs, one at a time, beating well after each addition. Beat in vanilla and water. Combine flour, baking soda and salt; gradually add to the creamed mixture. Drop by heaping tablespoons 2 in. apart onto ungreased baking sheets. Flatten with a fork. Bake at 350° for 12-15 minutes or until golden brown. Remove to wire racks to cool. **Yield:** about 18 dozen. **Editor's Note:** This recipe can be halved to fit into a mixing bowl.

Chocolate Chip Crispies

Stephanie DiGiovanni, Wakefield, Massachusetts

In this recipe from a cousin, potato chips add crunch while oats make them chewy. It's a fun twist to traditional chocolate chip cookies.

- 1 cup butter *or* margarine, softened
- 1 cup vegetable oil
- 1 cup sugar
- 1 cup packed brown sugar
- 1 egg
- 1 teaspoon vanilla extract
- 3-1/2 cups all-purpose flour
- 1 cup quick-cooking oats
- 1 teaspoon baking soda
- 1 teaspoon cream of tartar
- 1/2 teaspoon salt
- 1 tablespoon milk
- 1 teaspoon vinegar
- 2 cups (12 ounces) semisweet chocolate chips
- 1 cup crushed potato chips

In a large mixing bowl, cream butter, oil and sugars. Beat in egg and vanilla. Combine flour, oats, baking soda, cream of tartar and salt; gradually add to the

creamed mixture. Combine milk and vinegar; add to creamed mixture. Stir in chocolate chips and potato chips. Drop by tablespoonfuls 2 in. apart onto ungreased baking sheets. Bake at 350° for 12-15 minutes or until golden brown. Remove to wire racks to cool. **Yield:** about 8 dozen.

Big-Batch Butterscotch Cookies

JoAnne Riechman, McComb, Ohio

My mom and I perfected this recipe years ago. We get rave reviews on these crowd-pleasing cookies.

- 1-1/2 cups butter *or* margarine, softened
- 3 cups packed brown sugar
- 3 eggs
- 1 tablespoon vanilla extract
- 5-1/4 cups all-purpose flour
- 1 tablespoon baking powder
- 1-1/2 teaspoons baking soda
- 1/2 teaspoon cream of tartar

In a large mixing bowl, cream the butter and brown sugar. Add eggs, one at a time, beating well after each addition. Beat in vanilla. Transfer to a larger bowl if necessary. Combine flour, baking powder, baking soda and cream of tartar; gradually add to the creamed mixture. Drop by level tablespoonfuls 2 in. apart onto ungreased baking sheets. Bake at 350° for 10-12 minutes or until golden brown. Remove to wire racks to cool. **Yield:** about 20 dozen.

Michigan Cherry Drops

Carol Blue, Barnesville, Pennsylvania

I usually double this recipe so that I have plenty to share during the holidays. Pretty pink cookies such as these are a wonderful treat.

- 1 cup butter *or* margarine, softened
- 1 cup sugar
- 1/2 cup packed brown sugar
- 4 eggs
- 1-1/2 teaspoons vanilla extract
- 4 cups all-purpose flour
- 1 teaspoon salt
- 1 teaspoon ground cinnamon
- 1/2 teaspoon ground nutmeg
- 3-1/2 cups chopped walnuts
- 3 cups chopped maraschino cherries
- 2-2/3 cups raisins

In a large mixing bowl, cream the butter and sugars. Add eggs, one at a time, beating well after each addition. Beat in vanilla. Combine flour, salt, cinnamon and nutmeg; gradually add to the creamed mixture.

Transfer to a larger bowl if necessary. Stir in walnuts, cherries and raisins. Drop by tablespoonfuls 2 in. apart onto ungreased baking sheets. Bake at 350° for 16-18 minutes or until lightly browned. Remove to wire racks to cool. Store in an airtight container. **Yield:** about 14 dozen.

Cornflake Crisps

Andrea Basped, Patuxent River, Maryland

With oats, coconut, nuts, and butterscotch and chocolate chips, there's something for everyone in this cookie. It's my mom's recipe.

>   2 cups butter *or* margarine, softened
>   2 cups sugar
>   2 cups packed brown sugar
>   4 eggs
>   2 teaspoons vanilla extract
>   4 cups all-purpose flour
>   2 teaspoons baking powder
>   2 teaspoons baking soda
>   2 cups quick-cooking oats
>   2 cups cornflakes
>   1 cup flaked coconut
>   1 cup chopped pecans
>   1 cup *each* butterscotch, semisweet and milk chocolate chips

In a large mixing bowl, cream the butter and sugars. Add eggs, one at a time, beating well after each addition. Beat in vanilla. Combine flour, baking powder and baking soda; gradually add to creamed mixture. Transfer to a larger bowl if necessary. Add remaining ingredients; mix well. Drop by tablespoonfuls 3 in. apart onto ungreased baking sheets. Bake at 350° for 12-14 minutes or until golden brown. Remove to wire racks to cool. **Yield:** 9 dozen.

Oatmeal Raisin Cookies

Sandi Swartzenberger, Kalispell, Montana

In my small neighborhood, my grandkids and their friends stop by throughout the day. I keep my cookie jar well supplied with these.

>   2 cups butter *or* margarine, softened
>   2 cups packed brown sugar
>   1 cup sugar
>   2 eggs
>   1/2 cup water
>   2 teaspoons vanilla extract
>   6 cups quick-cooking oats
> 2-1/2 cups all-purpose flour
>   2 teaspoons salt

>   2 teaspoons ground cinnamon
>   1 teaspoon baking soda
> 2-1/2 cups raisins
>   2 cups (12 ounces) semisweet chocolate chips
> 1-1/2 cups chopped walnuts
>   1 cup flaked coconut

In a large mixing bowl, cream the butter and sugars. Add eggs, one at a time, beating well after each addition. Beat in water and vanilla. Combine the oats, flour, salt, cinnamon and baking soda; gradually add to creamed mixture. Transfer to a larger bowl if necessary. Stir in raisins, chocolate chips, walnuts and coconut. Drop by level tablespoonfuls 2 in. apart onto ungreased baking sheets. Bake at 350° for 12-14 minutes or until lightly browned. Remove to wire racks to cool. **Yield:** about 12-1/2 dozen.

Surprise Crinkles

Lola Fensky, Moundridge, Kansas

I created this recipe by trial and error using many different kinds of candy. Milky Ways were the secret "surprise" my family liked best.

>   1 cup shortening
>   1/2 cup butter *or* margarine, softened
>   2 cups packed brown sugar
>   1 cup sugar
>   3 eggs
> 1-1/2 teaspoons vanilla extract
> 4-1/4 cups all-purpose flour
> 1-1/2 teaspoons baking soda
>   1/4 teaspoon ground cinnamon
>   1/8 teaspoon salt
>   2 packages (14 ounces *each*) fun-size Milky Way candy bars

In a large mixing bowl, cream the shortening, butter and sugars. Add eggs, one at a time, beating well after each addition. Beat in vanilla. Combine flour, baking soda, cinnamon and salt; gradually add to the creamed mixture. Roll into 1-1/2-in. balls. Cut each candy bar into fourths; push one portion into the center of each ball, completely covering candy with dough. Place 2 in. apart on ungreased baking sheets. Bake at 350° for 12-14 minutes or until golden brown and surface cracks. Remove to wire racks to cool. **Yield:** 9 dozen.

TO FREEZE drop cookie dough, drop the dough as recipe directs onto a baking sheet and freeze until solid. Remove to a heavy-duty resealable plastic bag. When ready to bake, let thaw on a baking sheet at room temperature for about 30 minutes before baking.

Nut-Filled Horns

Penny Field, Waynesboro, Virginia

"Simply the best" is what most folks say after sampling these rich, flaky cookies. It's a thrill to share them with friends and family during the holidays.

2 cups butter *or* margarine, softened
2 packages (8 ounces *each*) cream cheese, softened
2 egg yolks
4-1/2 cups all-purpose flour
2 teaspoons baking powder
FILLING:
4 cups finely chopped walnuts
1-1/2 to 2 cups sugar
6 tablespoons evaporated milk
1-1/2 teaspoons vanilla extract

In a large mixing bowl, cream the butter and cream cheese. Add egg yolks. Combine flour and baking powder; gradually add to the creamed mixture. Cover and chill overnight. Combine filling ingredients in a bowl (mixture will be thick). Divide dough into fourths (dough will be sticky). On a well-sugared surface, roll out each portion into a 12-in. x 10-in. rectangle. Cut into 2-in. squares. Place about 1 teaspoon filling in the center of each square. Fold over two opposite corners; seal tightly. Place 2 in. apart on ungreased baking sheets. Bake at 350° for 15-18 minutes or until lightly browned. Remove to wire racks to cool. **Yield:** 10 dozen.

Oatmeal Molasses Crisps

Jori Schellenberger, Everett, Washington

In Amish and Mennonite homes, home cooking is guaranteed delicious. So when I found this recipe in an Amish cookbook, I knew I had to try it. It's become a favorite of our family as well as the folks at our church fellowship.

2-1/2 cups butter *or* margarine, softened
5 cups sugar
4 eggs
1/3 cup dark molasses
1 tablespoon vanilla extract
4-1/3 cups all-purpose flour
4 teaspoons baking powder
3 teaspoons ground cinnamon
2 teaspoons salt
1 teaspoon baking soda
4-3/4 cups old-fashioned oats
2 cups finely chopped pecans

In a large mixing bowl, cream butter and sugar. Add eggs, one at a time, beating well after each addition. Beat in molasses and vanilla. Combine the flour, baking powder, cinnamon, salt and baking soda; gradually add to the creamed mixture. Transfer to a larger bowl if necessary. Stir in oats and pecans. Drop by tablespoonfuls 2 in. apart onto greased baking sheets. Bake at 375° for 8-10 minutes or until edges are firm. Cool for 3 minutes before removing to wire racks. **Yield:** 15 dozen.

Soft Apple Butter Delights

Shirley Harter, Greenfield, Indiana

I won first place at a local apple bake-off with this original recipe. I especially like to take these hearty cookies to gatherings in fall.

1 cup butter *or* margarine, softened
2 cups packed brown sugar
2 eggs
1/2 cup brewed coffee, room temperature
3-1/2 cups all-purpose flour
1 teaspoon baking soda
1 teaspoon salt
1 teaspoon ground nutmeg
2 cups apple butter*
1 cup chopped walnuts

In a large mixing bowl, cream the butter and brown sugar. Add eggs, one at a time, beating well after each addition. Beat in coffee. Combine flour, baking soda, salt and nutmeg; gradually add to the creamed mixture. Stir in apple butter and walnuts (dough will be soft). Refrigerate for 1 hour. Drop by teaspoonfuls 2 in. apart onto lightly greased baking sheets. Bake at 400° for 10-12 minutes or until edges are firm. Remove to wire racks to cool. **Yield:** 10 dozen.
*Editor's Note: This recipe was tested with commercially prepared apple butter.

Monster Cookies

Dolores DeMarco, Hammonton, New Jersey

These big crisp cookies are packed with lots of irresistible ingredients, so they appeal to everyone. When you put a plate of these cookies on the table, they disappear in a flash.

2 cups butter *or* margarine, softened
2 cups sugar
2 cups packed brown sugar
4 eggs
4 teaspoons vanilla extract
3 cups all-purpose flour

2 teaspoons baking powder
1 teaspoon baking soda
4 cups quick-cooking oats
4 cups crisp rice cereal
2 cups flaked coconut
2 cups (12 ounces) semisweet chocolate chips
2 cups coarsely chopped walnuts

In a large mixing bowl, cream the butter and sugars. Add eggs, one at a time, beating well after each addition. Beat in vanilla. Combine flour, baking powder and baking soda; gradually add to the creamed mixture. Transfer to a larger bowl if necessary. Stir in the remaining ingredients. Drop by heaping tablespoonfuls 3 in. apart onto lightly greased baking sheets. Bake at 350° for 10-12 minutes or until golden brown. Remove to wire racks to cool. **Yield:** 8 dozen.

Crunchy Chip Cookies

Holly Diaz, Charleston, South Carolina

I frequently made these cookies when I was growing up and learning to cook. After recently rediscovering the recipe, making a batch and taking one bite, I quickly remembered how delicious they are!

1 cup butter *or* margarine, softened
1-1/2 cups packed brown sugar
1/2 cup sugar
2 eggs
1-1/2 teaspoons vanilla extract
2 cups all-purpose flour
1 teaspoon baking soda
1/2 teaspoon salt
2 cups quick-cooking oats
2 cups (12 ounces) semisweet chocolate chips
2 cups chow mein noodles
1/2 cup chopped pecans, toasted

In a large mixing bowl, cream the butter and sugars. Add eggs, one at a time, beating well after each addition. Beat in vanilla. Combine flour, baking soda and salt; gradually add to the creamed mixture. Stir in oats, chocolate chips, chow mein noodles and pecans. Drop by teaspoonfuls 2 in. apart onto lightly greased baking sheets. Bake at 350° for 10-12 minutes or until golden brown. Remove to wire racks to cool. **Yield:** about 12 dozen.

Butterscotch Banana Drops

Sonja Oberkramer, Pacific, Missouri

Most folks are surprised to learn that banana is the secret ingredient in these soft cookies. My grandmother shared the recipe with me some 30 years ago, and I've relied on it ever since.

3/4 cup butter *or* margarine, softened
1 cup sugar
1 egg
1-1/2 cups all-purpose flour
1/2 teaspoon salt
1/2 teaspoon baking soda
1/2 teaspoon ground nutmeg
1 cup mashed ripe bananas (about 2 medium)
1-1/2 cups quick-cooking oats
1-1/2 cups chopped pecans
1 cup butterscotch chips
1 cup chopped dates

In a large mixing bowl, cream butter and sugar. Beat in egg. Combine the flour, salt, baking soda and nutmeg; gradually add to the creamed mixture. Add bananas. Stir in oats, pecans, butterscotch chips and dates. Drop by rounded teaspoonfuls 2 in. apart onto lightly greased baking sheets. Bake at 350° for 12-14 minutes or until lightly browned. Remove to wire racks to cool. **Yield:** about 11 dozen.

Soft Ginger Cutouts

Connie Ellis, Sunapee, New Hampshire

I can still remember the wonderful aroma of spices wafting through our house while Mom baked these timeless cookies. They have a soft texture that melts in your mouth.

1-1/3 cups butter (no substitutes), softened
1 cup sugar
2 eggs
1 cup molasses
1/4 cup water
2 tablespoons vinegar
6 cups all-purpose flour
4 teaspoons baking soda
2 teaspoons ground ginger
1 teaspoon ground cinnamon
1/2 teaspoon salt

In a large mixing bowl, cream the butter and sugar. Add eggs, one at a time, beating well after each addition. Combine molasses, water and vinegar; add to the creamed mixture and mix until blended. Combine remaining ingredients; gradually add to the creamed mixture. Cover and refrigerate for 2 hours or until easy to handle. On a heavily floured surface, roll out dough to 1/4-in. thickness. Cut with a 2-1/2-in. cookie cutter dipped in flour. Place 1 in. apart on ungreased baking sheets. Bake at 350° for 10-12 minutes or until edges are browned. Remove to wire racks to cool. **Yield:** about 10 dozen.

Quick & Easy Treats

Peanut Butter Treats

Judy Stanton, Thonotosassa, Florida

(Pictured at left)

You can't miss with these no-fuss cookies. People are surprised to see the short list of ingredients. These cookies are fragile, so store them carefully when completely cooled.

>   2 cups peanut butter
> 1-1/4 cups sugar
>   2 eggs
>   52 milk chocolate stars *or* kisses

In a mixing bowl, cream peanut butter and sugar. Add eggs, one at a time, beating well after each addition (dough will be sticky). With floured hands, roll tablespoonfuls into 1-1/4-in. balls. Place 2 in. apart on ungreased baking sheets. Bake at 350° for 14-16 minutes or until tops are cracked. Remove to wire racks. Immediately press a chocolate star in the center of each. Cool. **Yield:** 4-1/2 dozen.

Quick Chocolate Sandwich Cookies

Mary Rempel, Altona, Manitoba

(Pictured at left)

 These cookies freeze well, so it's easy to keep some on hand for last-minute munching. In summer, I often make them larger to use for ice cream sandwiches.

>   2 packages (18-1/4 ounces *each*) devil's food
>   cake mix
>   1 cup vegetable oil
>   4 eggs
> **FILLING:**
>   1 package (8 ounces) cream cheese, softened
>   1/4 cup butter *or* margarine, softened
> 2-1/2 cups confectioners' sugar
>   1 teaspoon vanilla extract

In a mixing bowl, combine the cake mixes, oil and eggs; mix well. Roll into 1-in. balls. Place 2 in. apart on un-

---

greased baking sheets. Do not flatten. Bake at 350° for 8-10 minutes or until set. Cool for 5 minutes before removing to wire racks (cookies will flatten as they cool). In a small mixing bowl, beat cream cheese and butter. Add sugar and vanilla; beat until smooth. Spread on the bottom of half of the cookies; top with remaining cookies. Store in the refrigerator. **Yield:** about 6 dozen.

No-Bake Cereal Bars

Pauline Christiansen, Columbus, Kansas

(Pictured at left)

This big-batch recipe was given to me by a school cafeteria cook. I've made them for picnics and church activities too many times to count. They're favored by young and old alike.

>   2 cups sugar
>   2 cups corn syrup
>   1 jar (40 ounces) chunky peanut butter
>   6 cups Cheerios
>   6 cups crisp rice cereal

In a large saucepan, cook and stir sugar and corn syrup until the sugar is dissolved. Remove from the heat. Add peanut butter; mix well. Stir in cereals. Spread quickly into two lightly greased 15-in. x 10-in. x 1-in. pans. Cut into bars while warm. **Yield:** about 10 dozen.

Plantation Bars

Jeanette Pederson, Monico, Wisconsin

Instead of the typical melted marshmallows, this clever recipe calls for melted vanilla chips. With crisp rice cereal, peanut butter and nuts, these bars taste almost like candy.

>   2 packages (12 ounces *each*) vanilla chips
>   1 cup peanut butter
>   7 cups crisp rice cereal
>   1 cup salted peanuts

In a large microwave-safe bowl, combine the vanilla chips and peanut butter. Microwave, uncovered, on high for 2 minutes or until melted; stir until smooth. Stir in cereal and nuts. Press into a greased 13-in. x 9-in. x 2-in. pan. Refrigerate for 2 hours or until firm. Cut into bars. **Yield:** 3 dozen. **Editor's Note:** This recipe was tested in a 900-watt microwave.

> **SIMPLE SOLUTIONS.** Pictured at left, clockwise from upper left: Peanut Butter Treats, Quick Chocolate Sandwich Cookies and No-Bake Cereal Bars (all recipes on this page).

Chocolate Marshmallow Grahams

Lynnes Welch, Riverside, Washington

While working at a local Grange, I came up with these chocolaty bars to serve with coffee to weary travelers. Folks always came back for more…and for the recipe!

- 2 cups (12 ounces) semisweet chocolate chips
- 1 cup butter *or* margarine
- 1 cup peanut butter
- 1 teaspoon vanilla extract
- 2 cups crushed chocolate graham crackers (about 30 squares)
- 1 package (10-1/2 ounces) miniature marshmallows

In a large microwave-safe bowl, combine chocolate chips, butter and peanut butter. Cover and microwave on high for 2 minutes; stir until well blended. Stir in vanilla. Add cracker crumbs and marshmallows; stir until coated. Spread into a greased 13-in. x 9-in. x 2-in. pan. Cover and refrigerate for 1 hour or until firm. Cut into bars. **Yield:** 6-1/2 dozen. **Editor's Note:** This recipe was tested in a 900-watt microwave.

Orange Coconut Balls

Helen Youngers, Kingman, Kansas

When my mother first made these slightly sweet morsels years ago, we immediately fell in love with their unique flavor.

- 1 package (12 ounces) vanilla wafers, crushed
- 3/4 cup confectioners' sugar
- 3/4 cup flaked coconut
- 1/2 cup finely chopped pecans
- 1/2 cup orange juice concentrate
- Additional confectioners' sugar

In a large bowl, combine the first five ingredients. Roll into 1-in. balls, then roll in confectioners' sugar. Store in the refrigerator. Roll in additional confectioners' sugar before serving if desired. **Yield:** 4-1/2 dozen.

Saucepan Fudgies

Sheila Redwine, Kingfisher, Oklahoma

It's hard to eat just one of these bite-size brownies. My boys like them a lot, so I often have some frozen cookie dough shaped into balls ready to pop into the oven.

- 4 squares (1 ounce *each*) unsweetened chocolate

- 1/4 cup butter (no substitutes)
- 2 cups sugar
- 2 eggs
- 1 teaspoon vanilla extract
- 2 cups all-purpose flour
- 2 teaspoons baking powder
- 1/4 teaspoon salt
- 1/4 cup chopped pecans
- Confectioners' *or* granulated sugar

In a large heavy saucepan, melt chocolate and butter over low heat, stirring constantly. Remove from the heat and cool slightly. Stir in sugar. Add eggs, one at a time, beating well after each addition. Beat in vanilla. Combine the flour, baking powder and salt; gradually add to chocolate mixture. Stir in pecans. Refrigerate for 30 minutes or until easy to handle. Roll into 1-in. balls, then roll in sugar. Place 2 in. apart on ungreased baking sheets. Bake at 300° for 18-20 minutes or until edges are set and tops crack. Remove to wire racks to cool. **Yield:** about 6 dozen.

Flourless Peanut Butter Cookies

Margaret Forger, Norwalk, Connecticut

Next time your family begs you for a homemade treat, don't fret! With only three ingredients, you can have a batch of these cookies baking in mere minutes.

- 4 egg whites
- 2 cups peanut butter
- 1-2/3 cups sugar

In a mixing bowl, beat egg whites until stiff peaks form. In another bowl, combine peanut butter and sugar; fold in egg whites. Drop by heaping teaspoonfuls 2 in. apart onto lightly greased baking sheets. Flatten slightly with a fork. Bake at 325° for 15-20 minutes or until set. Remove to wire racks to cool. **Yield:** about 6-1/2 dozen.

Chocolate-Berry Bars

Grace Laird, Barker, Texas

I created this recipe by accident when I wanted to make Rice Krispie bars with dried fruit. All I had in my cupboard were dried cranberries and chocolate chips, so I tossed them in.

- 5-1/2 cups crisp rice cereal
- 1/2 cup semisweet chocolate chips
- 1/2 cup dried cranberries
- 1/4 cup wheat germ, toasted
- 1 package (10-1/2 ounces) miniature marshmallows

2 teaspoons vegetable oil
2 teaspoons milk

In a large bowl, combine cereal, chocolate chips, cranberries and wheat germ; set aside. In a large microwave-safe bowl, combine the marshmallows, oil and milk. Microwave, uncovered, on high for 1 minute; stir. Microwave 1 minute longer or until marshmallows are puffed and melted; stir until smooth. Pour over cereal mixture; stir until chips are melted. Spread into a lightly greased 13-in. x 9-in. x 2-in. pan. Cut into bars. **Yield:** about 1-1/2 dozen. **Editor's Note:** This recipe was tested in a 900-watt microwave.

Macaroon Melts

Ronni Fandrick, Paso Robles, California

These festive cookies are made in the microwave, keeping your oven free for other holiday baking. I sometimes top the cookies with chocolate bells instead of kisses.

1/2 cup butter *or* margarine
32 large marshmallows
1/2 teaspoon almond extract
4 cups cornflakes
1 cup flaked coconut
1/2 cup chopped almonds
1/4 cup quartered candied cherries
Chocolate kisses *or* whole candied cherries

In a large microwave-safe bowl, combine the butter, marshmallows and extract. Microwave, uncovered, on high for 2 minutes or until melted. In a bowl, combine the cornflakes, coconut, almonds and quartered cherries. Stir in marshmallow mixture until coated. Drop by tablespoonfuls onto waxed paper-lined baking sheets. Immediately press a chocolate kiss or candied cherry in the center of each. **Yield:** 4 dozen. **Editor's Note:** This recipe was tested in a 900-watt microwave.

Chocolate Waffle Cookies

Betty Hart, Hayden Lake, Idaho

I reach for this recipe when I need a special dessert that requires little fuss. The cookies are quickly made in a waffle iron and then spread with chocolate frosting.

3/4 cup sugar
1/2 cup butter *or* margarine, melted
2 eggs
1 teaspoon vanilla extract
1 cup all-purpose flour
4-1/2 teaspoons baking cocoa
Chocolate frosting

In a bowl, combine sugar, butter, eggs and vanilla. Combine flour and cocoa; gradually add to the sugar mixture. Drop tablespoonfuls of batter into each section of a preheated waffle iron. Bake according to manufacturer's directions. Remove carefully; cool on wire racks. Spread with chocolate frosting. **Yield:** about 2 dozen.

Chewy Peanut Butter Crisps

Lucy Garrett, Cedartown, Georgia

This flourless cookie successfully combines a chewy inside and crisp outside. Plus, chocolate and peanut butter is a classic combination that's hard to beat.

1 cup peanut butter
1 cup sugar
1/2 cup evaporated milk
4 teaspoons cornstarch
1/2 cup semisweet chocolate chips

In a mixing bowl, combine peanut butter and sugar. Stir in milk and cornstarch until smooth. Add chocolate chips. Drop by heaping teaspoonfuls 2 in. apart onto ungreased baking sheets. Bake at 350° for 12-15 minutes or until golden brown. Remove to wire racks to cool. **Yield:** 3-1/2 dozen. **Editor's Note:** This recipe does not contain flour.

Butter Mint Cookies

Anita Epitropou, Zion, Illinois

These delicate cookies with a touch of mint were a big hit when I made them for a party at work.

1 cup butter (no substitutes), softened
1/2 cup confectioners' sugar
1-1/2 teaspoons peppermint extract
1-3/4 cups all-purpose flour

In a mixing bowl, cream butter, sugar and extract. Gradually add the flour; mix well. Roll tablespoonfuls of dough into balls. Place 1 in. apart on ungreased baking sheets; flatten with a glass dipped in sugar. Bake at 350° for 12-14 minutes or until firm. Remove to wire racks to cool. **Yield:** 3 dozen.

WHEN YOU'RE IN A PINCH, dress up store-bought cookies by dipping half of each cookie into melted chocolate and then in toasted coconut, chopped nuts or chocolate sprinkles.

INDEX